LISTS
FOR LIFE

LISTS FOR LIFE

THE ESSENTIAL GUIDE TO GETTING ORGANIZED AND TACKLING TOUGH TO-DOS

RORY TAHARI

SSE

Simon Spotlight Entertainment
New York

S|S|E

Simon Spotlight Entertainment
A Division of Simon & Schuster, Inc.
1230 Avenue of the Americas
New York, NY 10020

First Simon Spotlight Entertainment
trade paperback edition September 2009

SIMON SPOTLIGHT ENTERTAINMENT and colophon
are trademarks of Simon & Schuster, Inc.

For information about special discounts for
bulk purchases, please contact Simon & Schuster
Special Sales at 1-866-506-1949 or
business@simonandschuster.com.

The Simon & Schuster Speakers Bureau can bring
authors to your live event. For more information or
to book an event contact the Simon & Schuster
Speakers Bureau at 1-866-248-3049 or
visit our website at www.simonspeakers.com.

Designed by Davina Mock-Maniscalco

Manufactured in the United States of America

1   3   5   7   9   10   8   6   4   2

Library of Congress Cataloging-in Publication Data
Tahari, Rory.
Lists for life : the essential guide to getting organized
and tackling tough-to-dos / Rory Tahari.
p.   cm.
Includes bibliographies.
1. Life skills—Handbooks, manuals, etc.
2. Orderliness.   I. Title.
HQ2037.T344   2009
646.7—dc22   2009025518

ISBN 978-1-4391-2468-0
ISBN 978-1-4391-5357-4 (ebook)

NOTE TO READERS

This publication contains the opinions and ideas of its author. It is intended to provide helpful and informative material on the subjects addressed in the publication. It is sold with the understanding that the author and publisher are not engaged in rendering any personal professional services in the book. For many of the topics covered, you will need to consult with a professional, such as a doctor or a real estate, employment, or other attorney (particularly since applicable laws may vary from state to state).

In addition, this book sometimes recommends particular products, books, or services for your reference. The author is not affiliated in any way with such products or the companies that produce them. In all instances, bear in mind that there are items other than those recommended here that you may find useful.

The author and publisher specifically disclaim all responsibility for any liability, loss, or risk, personal or otherwise, which is incurred as a consequence, directly or indirectly, of the use and application of any of the contents of this book.

For Jeremey and Zoe—may you never need these lists and instead call me. I love you both more than anything in the world and hope that you, too, follow your dreams.

Mom and Dad, thank you for making me who I am today. Dad, you taught me to work hard. Mom, you taught me how to be organized. I love you both—the same amount. Now stop torturing me.

Josh, thank you for always making me laugh . . . and always demonstrating the moral high ground. Brittany, never forget that we have the best family in the world.

Elie, you challenged me every step of the way and I am forever grateful for it. You are a man of dreams and have shown me how to make all of mine come true. Without you, none of this would have been possible. Thank you for everything.

CONTENTS

INTRODUCTION

I have been a compulsive list maker since I was old enough to write. Some detractors might suggest the word *obsessive*, but I like to think that I am highly functioning and efficient. Other list-obsessed women I'm aware of (Madonna) seem to back up my claim. In any case, from the packing list I compiled for summer camp as an eleven-year-old to the college application checklist I already have handy for my kids (who are all under the age of ten), I like to deal with life's challenges one step at a time.

For years, I was a personal resource library for friends and family who needed information. The minute someone got pregnant, engaged, bought a house, or experienced any other milestone, my phone would start ringing. I was always happy to dash off a list and was proud that my checklists were helping others navigate life. When I started getting calls from friends of friends asking me to share my checklists for life's difficult moments, I realized it was time to go public.

So here it is.

This book isn't a beach read; it's not chick lit. Instead, it's more of an owner's manual for some of life's biggest events and transitions.

Keep it on the shelf with your reference books, in the kitchen near your day calendar, by your bedside, or anywhere that's handy. When you find yourself in need of a road map, tear out the appropriate chapter, tape it to your computer, and let me help you break down an overwhelming or challenging situation, step by step. I know that sometimes the toughest part of tackling a to-do can be figuring out how to get started, and I hope that the following checklists, resources, action items, and suggestions will have you on your way to a more organized and less stressful life.

LISTS
FOR LIFE

WEDDING

Did he ask? Did you ask? Was there a father with a shotgun involved? No matter, you're getting married! After you've properly celebrated your news and shared it with your loved ones, it is important to remember that planning your special day should *not* send you into couples therapy. And while the main points on the to-do list may seem obvious (invites, food, music), designating someone in advance to be on the sidelines with extra hose and a sewing kit could spell the difference between stressful and sublime.

Immediate To-Dos

1 Go to the bookstore or get online and buy the following books. They are the best reference guides for everything you will need to know and do to plan a great wedding.

> *The Knot Complete Guide to Weddings in the Real World,* by Carley Roney

> *The Complete Wedding Planner & Organizer,* by Elizabeth and Alex Lluch

2 Go to www.theknot.com to get a sense of what planning will entail. It is not only a comprehensive site, but also a great place to join forums, ask questions, and get ideas. See page 31 for additional online resources.

3 Go to the office supply store and purchase a tabbed file containing plastic inserts. Tabs should represent the different event elements (Caterer, Florist, Dress, and so on) and inserts will contain the written notes, magazine clippings, material samples, and anything else you want to save for each category. Post-it notes and small notepads will also be useful.

4 Buy bridal magazines (see page 31 for a list of recommendations) and start tearing out everything you see that you like (dresses, hairstyles, cakes, et cetera). Keep a file of everything. You will need these for future reference. They are also great tools when working with vendors.

Initial Planning

1 Figure out how many people you want to invite. This will drive every decision you make and determine what your wedding will cost. This is the most important decision you can make. (Tip: My rule of thumb: Invite only the people you feel confident you will know in ten years. Everyone must love you both and be happy for you both! Otherwise you are going to look back at your photos and wonder, *Why did I invite them?*)

2 Pick a date but be prepared to have a back-up date if your wedding location of choice isn't available. Bear in mind that holidays will require you to give your guests more advance notice for dates, hotel and travel bookings, and other arrangements.

3 Set a budget (see page 6).

4 Book vendors (see page 7 on how to deal with them).

5 Type up a list of names and addresses of invitees and start tracking down missing addresses immediately. This will take more time than you think. Let your parents and future in-laws know how many people they can invite so they can work on their lists and give them back to you in your allotted time frame.

6 Make sure you spell every guest's name correctly. Have someone proofread your guest list for errors. People are easily offended if their names are spelled wrong.

7 Pick one address (and one phone number and/or email address) that you and your fiancé(e) are going to use for all wedding correspondence. Ensure that this one will be valid during the entire planning process and for at least two months after your wedding. If you can't use a personal address, then get a post office box so RSVPs and gifts don't go missing.

8 Send out your "save the date" cards. Important to note: Send these out six months in advance for weddings that will take place in the summer, on a holiday weekend, or at a special destination.

9 Secure a block of hotel rooms for your guests and try to negotiate a discounted rate. Do this at more than one hotel, so that your guests have a choice, to accommodate different budgets.

10 If you wish to incorporate any special religious traditions or ceremonies into your service, speak with your priest, rabbi, or clergyman about potential restrictions, rules, and other important details.

11 Create a spreadsheet for keeping track of all the thank-you notes you'll have to write. As gifts arrive, log the name of the sender, date received, and gift. Be detailed, in case you receive the same item but in different colors, sizes, et cetera.

12 Register for gifts. You might even want to register before sending your save-the-date cards because people sometimes start giving gifts as soon as they hear you are engaged.

Info for Your Guests

Everyone you know will be calling and asking you questions about the wedding (where to stay, where to eat, what time pictures are being taken). You may be surprised by how annoying these phone calls can be, especially since you will be busy and nervous about the big day. I suggest that you prepare an informational email guide for your guests and send it to them around the time that you send

→

your save-the-date cards. Alternatively, you can post information to a wedding website and include the address for the site on your save-the-date cards. (You can do this a number of ways. Many wedding-related websites offer templates that are very user-friendly.) Then, when guests call with questions, simply say, "I emailed you the information!" or "Go on our website!"

Info to Include

• *Most important:* A point person, preferably other than you (complete with their name and contact info), who guests can contact if they have questions

• Whether or not children are welcome at the wedding

• Date and time of your rehearsal dinner (if applicable), wedding ceremony, and reception

• Location of ceremony (be sure to include the zip code)

• Location of reception (if different from ceremony)

• Driving directions to ceremony and reception

• Parking near wedding venue and reception

• Hotels (in all price ranges). If you have a block of rooms, this is the place to give information regarding rates, availability, and deadlines to book.

• A list of the nearest airports

$\longrightarrow$

- Restaurants; include a brief description of each

- Activities for your guests

- Spa, hair, and nail salons (women will want to know where to go)

- Transportation; phone numbers for cab or car rental companies

- Dry cleaners

Setting a Budget

1 Determine the number of guests, then call all vendors and ask for approximate costs per person.

2 Negotiate with your vendors. The initial price offered is just a starting point. Most people don't realize this and end up paying "sticker price." Vendors expect you to negotiate.

3 Decide how you will pay for the wedding and how much you can afford to spend. (It will likely cost anywhere from $150 to $300 per person.) For some reason a good friend of mine overlooked this calculation and was overwhelmed by how much it ended up costing. Don't make the same mistake. Here is a rough breakdown of where your money will go.

45% Reception (location fee plus food)

12% Flowers

10% Entertainment, Music (DJ, musicians)

10% Photography, Videography

8% Attire (tuxedos, *not* including the bride's dress)

2% Ceremony

2% Stationery (save the date, invitations, thank-you notes, postage)

2% Wedding rings

2% Parking, transportation (for entire wedding party)

2% Gifts

5% Miscellaneous

In addition to the wedding, consider funds for the following, which amount to $10,000 to $35,000 extra!

Wedding dress ($1,000 to $10,000)

Rehearsal dinner ($2,000 to $10,000)

Honeymoon ($5,000 to $10,000)

Brunch the day after the wedding for out-of-town guests ($2,000 to $5,000)

Working with Vendors

1 Write in every contract that all fees are included in the final price they give you. Vendors are notorious for adding fees *after* the wedding is over. Be sure to explicitly state that you will *not* pay anything that they try to bill you for after the fact.

2 Type up a contact list of all vendors you will be using and email the list to all your vendors. This way, if they need to get in touch with

one another, they can do so without having to go through you. Encourage all of them to communicate openly, so that everyone will be in the loop.

3 Enter dates of when payments are due for your vendors on your calendar so everyone gets paid on time. Paying them late is a bad idea, because they will not be motivated to do a good job. Pay special attention to exchange rates if you're working with vendors abroad.

Location

1 Once you have picked your vendors, speak to the person in charge at your reception location and ask if there's anything special that you need to communicate to your vendors on their behalf (e.g., do not roll equipment on the dance floor, what time the location will become available for setup).

2 Type all of the information you learned during that conversation in one document and email it to your vendors so you have a paper trail that proves you communicated these needs. Send with an email notification back to you when the recipient opens and/or reads your email.

3 Be sure to also follow up with a phone call to your vendors. Make sure they received and reviewed the information. You wouldn't believe how often important information ends up in spam folders.

FLORIST:
GENERAL LIST OF FLORAL NEEDS

Bride's bouquet

Bridesmaids' bouquets

Groom's and groomsmen's boutonnieres

Parents' and grandparents' boutonnieres, corsages

Flower girl's bouquet, pomander

Ceremony décor (e.g., flowers for aisles)

Cocktail table arrangements

Dinner arrangements (centerpieces, arrangements on food tables)

General decorations (ask your florist for ideas)

Restroom arrangements

Rehearsal dinner décor

In-room arrangements for special guests

Lighting, which is sometimes provided by the florist (candles, twinkle lights). I think lighting is one of the most important event elements, so you might want to consider hiring someone in addition to your florist to handle this area.

Tip: Be sure to bring examples torn from magazines of arrangements you like when you meet with your florist. It's a good idea to bring a couple of options, because many times flowers are out of season. Also, ask the florist to show you photos from other weddings they serviced. This will let you know what to expect.

Photographer and Videographer

1 Ask to see the photographer's portfolio so you can get an idea of what kind of pictures you like. Be sure to point out your favorites to the photographer so you can try to get the same type of photographs. For example, I loved the idea of taking black-and-white documentary-style photos before the wedding, when I was getting dressed. This idea was taken from a picture I saw in a magazine of a bride staring out the window.

2 Tell your parents to send you a list of pictures that they want to have. They *will* have opinions, and you are better off asking in advance than dealing with their disappointment later. For example, my mother wanted to make sure she got a photo of herself with all her sisters. They rarely were all together in one place and it was important to her.

3 Make a complete list of all the different pictures you want taken and send the list to the photographer. This is called a "shot list." Think of this as a blueprint for what the photographers will shoot. Share this list with anyone important to you, so you can get feedback for more ideas or to see if you missed anyone important. Consider giving your maid of honor (or another responsible guest) a copy of the shot list to ensure that the list is followed on the day of the wedding. Assign someone the responsibility of checking in with the photographer during the event to be sure nothing is overlooked.

4 Give your photographer and/or videographer a contact person for the day of the

wedding to answer their questions. It is not fun fielding questions from your photographer and videographer during the wedding.

5 Type up and give your photographer a time-line of events so they know what is happening and when. That way they should get every moment on film. My videographer was in the bathroom when my mother got up and sang us a song. To this day, my mother is still upset about it.

6 Consider taking your family portraits before the ceremony. It takes so much longer than you would expect, and if you do it after the ceremony, you will be missing out on your party! No matter what you decide, set a time limit for how long you want to take photos, or you may be there all night.

7 If you are hiring a videographer, be sure to discuss how you want the event to be shot. Do you want taping to be unobtrusive? Do you want the videographers walking around and interviewing guests? Do you want them to set up in a corner and whoever wants to be interviewed can come over? My videographer was practically part of the ceremony. All the guests complained, but ten years later I can tell you my kids are happy because they can watch and feel like they're right there in the front row.

8 If your photographer is shooting film (not digital), tell him to number the proofs; it makes ordering prints much easier.

9 Tell the photographer you want to own the negatives. That way you can print them as often as you like without any additional costs.

(Photographers make the bulk of their money printing the photos.)

10 Ask for images to be posted on the photographer's website so your friends and family members can order prints easily directly through the site.

Caterer

1 Consider having your cocktail hour before the ceremony. Guests are always running late, and this gives them an earlier time to aim for (plus a chance to relax, have a drink, and then enjoy the wedding).

2 Request a tasting at least three weeks before your wedding so you can decide what food you like. Let your caterer know that whatever they present to you at your food tasting should be available on your menu.

3 At the tasting, preview a sample of a complete place setting and approve all serving and table items (plates, trays, flatware, glasses, tablecloth, napkins).

4 If you are having a buffet, consider having "open seating" and letting your guests sit wherever they want. They will naturally gravitate toward whom they want to sit with, and this saves you the pressure of having to decide on seating arrangements. Of all the things I did, my guests probably appreciated this most.

5 Specify if you want a certain type of alcohol served during dinner.

6 Find out well in advance if anyone attending the wedding has dietary needs (e.g., nut allergies, vegetarian, kosher) and tell your caterer as soon as possible. If your guests tell the caterer during the wedding they need something special, the caterer will charge you extra. (It's always a good idea to have vegetarian options on the menu regardless, in case you are unaware of any dietary needs ahead of time.)

7 Have your caterer put in writing anything that would be considered an extra charge that is not included in the quoted price (e.g., cake-cutting fee, taxes, tips). This way you have a realistic idea of what the "real" cost is going to be.

8 Show the person who is designing your wedding cake photos of how you want your cake to look.

9 If your caterer is running a coat check, make sure there are enough people assigned to check in and release coats.

Entertainment

1 Try to schedule a visit to hear the band or DJ you are hiring when they are playing at an event. It will give you a much better idea of how they'll perform at your reception than listening to a recording.

2 Put in the contract how much time your band or DJ gets for breaks and when. You want to know how long they will play continuously. Also, find out what recorded music they put on while they take their breaks. You want to make sure it goes with the tone of your wedding.

3 Ask your band/DJ/ceremony musicians to fax you a list of their most commonly requested songs. This will help give you ideas for the following:

> Processional (when your wedding party is walking down the aisle)
>
> Bridal procession (when the bride is walking)
>
> Recessional (when you are walking back as a married couple after the ceremony)
>
> First dance
>
> Second dance

4 Listen to your musicians do an actual rendition of the important songs (ceremony, first dance). The same song can be played multiple ways, and theirs may not be your tempo of choice. You don't want surprises during important moments.

5 Keep a notebook with you at all times to take down names of any songs you hear that you may want to include in your wedding. Equally important: Songs you may wish to avoid.

6 Avoid putting together band members who have not played together.

7 Allow the band to do what they do best. If you provide them with lots of songs they don't know, they may not play them well.

8 Discuss attire for the band. Otherwise, some band members may wear inappropriate or unattractive outfits.

Transportation

1 Book arrangements for you to get to the wedding *and* get home. Everyone thinks about getting to the event; no one ever thinks about getting home. I ended up walking home after my wedding!

2 Be aware of others' transportation needs. Most out-of-town guests will need transportation and will need help organizing it. Find out if the hotel where you blocked off rooms has a low-cost shuttle for your guests. If so, reserve it.

3 If you and your fiancé(e) are going to be using your cars to get to the ceremony but plan on leaving your reception in a limo, ask someone in advance if they can drive you to pick up your cars the next day. Or, if you can, arrange for a friend or family member to drive them home after the event.

Dress

1 Bring the shoes and undergarments (underwear, bra, corset) you will be wearing on the wedding day to each fitting.

2 Bring someone to a fitting who will be honest with you about how your dress looks. Be open-minded!

3 Request and schedule a third fitting. Shops normally only include two fittings in the price. The third fitting is worth it if you have to pay extra. You do not want to wear a dress that's too big or too small on your wedding day.

Note: Be aware that some dresses take six months or more to make.

Registering

1 Register as soon as possible. Some people will start giving you gifts immediately after they hear you are engaged. You don't want to end up with gifts you don't want.

2 Find out if the store will allow you to return items and apply the credit in different departments. (e.g., Can you return a vase and put the money toward new towels?).

3 Go to the store and see items in person before you register for online. Photos on websites can be deceiving.

4 Decide where and when you want all your items to be shipped. You might want to consider shipping certain items to your parents, for example, if you do not have room for them in your home. Or you may decide to have your gifts delivered after you return from your honeymoon.

5 Register for fun items as well as items you need.

6 Order or purchase thank-you notes as soon as you register at the first store.

Marriage License: What You Will Need

Note: Requirements may vary from state to state, but this should give you some sense of what to expect. I recommend calling the licensing office or visiting their website well in advance so you'll know what to bring and be aware of any restrictions.

For the bride and groom:

• Birth certificate. You will likely need an original or certified copy of your birth certificate to get your marriage license (a regular photocopy may not suffice).

• Driver's license

• Passport (or proof of citizenship)

• Proof of divorce (if there was a previous marriage)

Important to know: You must have all of the above for *both bride and groom*. Make sure nothing has expired or is about to expire! Also, bear in mind:

Once you get the license, it may be valid for only a limited period.

There may be a waiting period after receiving the license before you can get married.

IF YOU ARE A FRIEND OR FAMILY MEMBER OF THE BRIDE OR GROOM (THE GOLDEN RULES)

1. Be as helpful as possible. From the minute your friend or family member is engaged, you should only say, "How can I help?" and try to keep your opinion to yourself (unless asked for it).

2. RSVP on time for every event.

3. Don't take things personally. Remember, *it's not about you!*

4. Show up on time for all events whether it's an appointment for getting your hair done or the rehearsal dinner. There is nothing worse than being the bride and having to chase down your friends or family on the big day.

5. Check all your wedding gear when you pick up your items (shoes, dress, rental tux, bouquet). Inspect them to make sure you have everything you need and they're in good condition. No bride or groom wants to hear, "There is a problem with your stuff!"

6. During photographs, be ready and alert. Don't drift off to another location.

7. If your children are in the bridal party, it is your job to "wrangle" them and make sure they are doing what they are supposed to do. It is not the bride or groom's responsibility.

8. If you bring kids to the wedding, it is your job to watch them.

9. Don't be offended if your name is spelled wrong on place cards, programs, and other printed material.

10. Do not point out mistakes on the day of the wedding to your friend or a family mem-

ber of the couple. They want to focus on the wonderful things that day and not the things that went wrong. If it is something you can take care of, then do it. If not, forget it!

11. If you are a friend of the bride, your motto should be, "I do what I'm told." She will remember those who loved her and helped her and hate those who just worried about themselves.

12. Don't try to direct the band or photographers unless you are specifically asked to do so by the bride. It can be upsetting for the bride to have a friend or family member ask for their favorite song to be played.

13. Offer to show your speech to the groom and/or the bride before the big day; they might want to review it.

Week Before the Wedding

1 Make a list of every vendor you will need to tip and get enough cash together to cover the costs (most vendors do not take checks on the wedding day). Keep the cash in an envelope in a safe place until you give it to your designated tipper on the big day.

2 Schedule facials and waxing appointments for several days before your wedding. You do not want any skin irritations the day before.

3 Men: Do not shave for a few days prior to your wedding. That way you will get the cleanest shave on the day of the wedding.

4 Pick up all final wedding clothing (dress, shoes, tuxedo) and make sure it fits!

5 Start packing for the day of the wedding (see checklist, page 22) and honeymoon.

6 Read "Day-of" to-dos. Give necessary assignments and make all necessary arrangements.

7 Apply self-tanner.

8 Get your teeth whitened.

9 Touch up your hair color and cut one last time pre-wedding.

10 Do a trial run with your hair stylist and makeup artist so you'll look exactly how you want to look on the big day.

Day-of

1 Assign the following to-dos to friends or family members:

> Assign *one* person the task of gathering and keeping track of all important items (marriage license, wedding rings).

> Assign someone to answer the phone at your house and your cell phone.

> Give one person your personal camera and ask them to take pictures, so the next day you can see the photos.

> Put one person in charge of the cash to tip vendors. Give them a list of the vendors they will need to tip and exact amounts.

Assign one person in your bridal group whom you can call with any changes of plans. Then *they* can be responsible for spreading the word via a phone chain. Be sure this person has a contact list of all the people to call.

Have a friend or family member do a walk-through of the ceremony and reception locations to remove anything that you don't want to be in the photos. (My mother's best friend noticed a fire extinguisher that would have been in every one of my photos!)

2 Consider getting a massage.

3 Eat before your wedding; it's possible that you will not have one minute to eat later.

4 Have food in the bridal suite when people are getting ready. Someone is always hungry. Also, if possible, have food and drinks available during family pictures.

5 Print directions to all possible locations (guests often show up without any clue where to go). Have extra copies at each place, just in case someone loses theirs.

6 Tell the bridesmaids and groomsmen to arrive at an earlier time than is actually planned for photos so they will arrive on time.

7 Have a copy of the list of photos you want taken on hand.

8 If you are staying at a hotel that evening, make sure you drop off in advance anything

you will need at the hotel the morning after the wedding.

9 Set an auto-reply for your email.

10 Have someone bring a "wedding emergency kit" to the ceremony and reception sites. This should include stain removers for clothing, a mini sewing kit, Advil and Tylenol, Band-Aids, and anything else you might need on the big day. (You can buy these pre-made on the internet.) My best friend's zipper broke on her wedding dress the day of the wedding. We were in a small town in Greece, so there wasn't a drugstore in sight. The emergency kit I brought had safety pins, and it saved the day.

11 Ask someone close to you to come up to you during the wedding and say, "Stop, look around, pay attention, and enjoy every moment because the night will be over before you know it."

12 Consider sneaking off right after the ceremony with your spouse to have ten minutes alone before the reception. It is a special moment that you will never get to have again, and it feels good to take it all in together.

Wedding Day Packing List

MEDICINES

Advil

Aleve

Afrin

Antacid

Aspirin

Chloroseptic (You might need this sore throat spray after greeting your guests for hours.)

Tylenol

Note: Be sure to bring any prescription drugs you're currently taking and make sure you have enough to last throughout your honeymoon, if necessary.

TOILETRIES

Baby wipes (good for quick cleanup, and they take stains off clothing)

Band-Aids

ChapStick

Dental floss

Dental floss picks

Deodorant

Listerine Breath Strips (better for freshening up than a bride chewing gum!)

Tampons, pads

Tissues

Toothbrush

Toothpaste

Vaseline

HAIR ITEMS

Blow-dryer

Bobby pins

Hairbrush

Hair iron (for straightening)

Hair mousse, gel, spray

ELECTRONICS

Camera, battery, and film or extra memory cards

Cell phone and charger

Video camera and charger

BEAUTY NEEDS

Facial soap

Hand lotion

Hand sanitizer

Invisible blemish treatment

Makeup (for touch-ups)

Mirror

Nail file

Nail polish (clear)

Nail polish remover

Perfume and cologne

MISCELLANEOUS

Double-sided tape

Dr. Scholl's shoe inserts

Drinking straws (so you don't ruin your lipstick)

Energy bars

Flip-flops (to change into after the ceremony)

Iron (to get out last-minute wrinkles)

Large ziplock freezer bags (to store hair-pins and other items)

Lint remover

Mints

Pantyhose (spare pairs)

Safety pins

Scissors

Small sewing kit (or needle and thread)

Stain remover pens

Static remover spray

Super Glue

AND, OF COURSE, THE IMPORTANT THINGS

Gown

Shoes

Veil

Wedding rings

Tuxedo

Marriage license

Passports and tickets

Purse

Toasts (print several copies)

Undergarments

Suitcase for honeymoon (if you are leaving straight from the ceremony)

Wallet

Superstitions—In Addition to the Standard "Old, New, Borrowed, Blue"

- Clip a lock of your hair for the groom to carry in his pocket.

- Sew a penny into the seam of your gown for happiness throughout your life.

- Have the groom make a wish as he slides the ring on your finger.

- Dance every dance at your wedding, but save the first and last for each other.

Day After the Wedding

1 Call everyone you know and talk about the wedding. It is soooo much fun. Write down the stories they tell you. You might want to add them to your photo album or at least keep a record of what happened on your big day.

2 Ask your closest friends and family to email you photos they took.

3 Have someone go by the wedding location and pick up whatever is left behind (people *always* leave stuff behind). Assign this person to collect wedding items such as the bride's bouquet, which can be preserved; broken glass (from a Jewish wedding), which is considered good luck; place cards of bride and groom, speech notes, et cetera—these are all great keepsakes.

4 Have a dry cleaner pick up the dress and clean it for storage.

5 Donate your leftover wedding flowers to a charity or hospice.

Honeymoon Planning

1 Decide how long you want to be away. Take travel days into consideration (how long it will take to get to your destination).

2 Before you book your honeymoon, try to speak to someone you know who's been there and has relatively the same interests and tastes as you.

3 If you are leaving the country, check your passport to make sure it is valid and that it isn't going to expire until well after your honeymoon.

4 Do not change your name until after you get back from your honeymoon. Otherwise your travel documents may be inaccurate.

Two Weeks Before the Honeymoon To-Dos

1 Pay your bills in advance so when you are on your honeymoon you don't have to worry about finances.

2 If you are honeymooning abroad, tell your credit card companies and bank in advance. Otherwise, when they see charges from unusual places, they might freeze your accounts assuming that your credit card has been stolen.

3 Email at least one person (other than your spouse) your honeymoon itinerary in case of emergency.

4 Before you arrive, tell the hotel you are staying in that you will be on your honeymoon. They will most likely do something extra for you.

5 Endorse all the checks and deposit them with the cash you receive as gifts before you leave for your honeymoon. Checks can take up to two weeks to clear, and if you wait until after your honeymoon, it may be a month after your wedding before the money hits your account!

Post-Honeymoon

If you have decided to change your name, do so on the following (www.missnowmrs.com can help you save a ton of time):

> 401(k), IRA (call your HR department)
>
> Bank accounts: checking, savings (go to your bank)
>
> Car insurance (call your insurance broker)
>
> Car registration (DMV)
>
> Credit card (credit card companies)
>
> Disability insurance
>
> Driver's license (DMV)
>
> Employment records (call your HR department)
>
> Home owner's insurance (call your insurance broker)
>
> Leases (call your landlords or managing agents)
>
> Life insurance (call your insurance broker)

Loans (call your bank)

Medical insurance (call your health care provider)

Mortgage (call your bank)

Online subscription services, such as Netflix

Passport (go to the post office)

Phone company and cell phones

Property titles (call your real estate lawyer)

Social Security

Stocks (call your stockbroker)

Subscriptions (magazines, newspapers)

Tax returns (call your accountant)

Telephone listings (remember to call 411 and 555-1212, because they are separate companies)

Trusts, granted annuities (call your estate lawyer)

Utilities

Voter registration

Wills (call your estate lawyer)

Other Things to Consider

1 Create a new email address with your new name.

2 Order stationery with your new name on it.

3 Notify all your doctors of your new name and update your insurance information.

4 Consolidate financials (benefits, banking, et cetera). Note: Do not consolidate credit cards, otherwise you will lower your credit line.

5 Email friends and family your new mailing and contact info.

6 Review your photo proofs and get them back to your photographer within three months of your wedding.

7 Keep a list of all gifts received as you receive them. This is your master list for thank-you notes. Plus, when you get invited to the givers' weddings, you will be able to refer to this list and give them something similar. You will also need this in case you regift. You don't want to regift a present to the person who gave it to you!

8 Write your thank-you notes! They should not go out more than a month after your wedding. Try to send notes as you receive gifts rather than all at once, and don't wait to write them until after your honeymoon. You'll be over-whelmed!

RESOURCES

BOOKS

Bridal Bargains, by Denise and Alan Fields

The Complete Wedding Planner & Organizer, by Elizabeth and Alex Lluch

The Knot Complete Guide to Weddings in the Real World, by Carley Roney

The Knot Ultimate Wedding Planner, by Carley Roney

MAGAZINES

Elegant Bride

InStyle Weddings

Martha Stewart Weddings

WEBSITES

The Knot: www.theknot.com

Martha Stewart Weddings: marthastewart weddings.com

weddingchannel.com

HOME

Whether you live in a cozy apartment or are lord of a manor, the principles of "keeping house" are basically the same, just on a different scale. Many of us do not have a staff of elves to keep our humble abodes ticking like clockwork. Even if we did, having knowledge of how things work and need to be maintained will add years to the life of the property.

Homes, like cars and people, need regular tune-ups, checkups, maintenance, and adjustments. In this chapter, I have put together a month-by-month calendar of what you should be doing and when, so come November you are not stuck with a leaking roof because you forgot to clean out the gutters in October.

Maintaining your home is easy compared to moving there. I, for one, hate to move. In fact, I once considered obtaining squatters' rights to an apartment with an expiring lease, rather than packing up my belongings and relocating. But I have put aside my aversion to corrugated cardboard and packing tape to offer you a comprehensive guide to making your move as painless as possible.

From upkeep to uprooting, here is everything you need to know about home sweet home.

BUYING A HOME: FIRST THINGS FIRST

Buying a house is often the single biggest investment you will make in your lifetime. Let's examine some of the factors that go into the purchase.

HOME

1 Your budget. Sit down with a financial adviser or accountant to determine what you can and can't afford for a monthly payment plus expenses like utilities and home maintenance. How large will your down payment be? How much will you need for furnishings, repairs, and renovations? What are you looking for: a "starter" house or one you can stay in as your family grows? And consider this rule of thumb I learned: Whatever you think your budget is, lower it 10 to 15 percent as you will always need extra money for any additional "surprises" that may arise.

2 Location. Location. Location. Right now you are thinking about buying, but one day you will also want to sell. A good real estate buy will be in a great location with proximity to excellent schools, grocery stores, hospitals, and shopping. Also consider proximity to work and cultural interests as well as to family and friends.

3 Financing. If you just won the lottery, you can pay all cash; otherwise you will need a mortgage. I recommend looking into financing before you start your search so you can make sure that you qualify ahead of time. Then, when you make your offer, you can have a preapproval letter on hand. Here are things to consider when securing a mortgage:

One of the first things you should do before attempting to secure a mortgage is obtain a copy of your credit report to see your credit score and correct any errors. Do not apply for a mortgage until you are sure everything is correct.

Do your homework. There are numerous types of loans and mortgages to choose from. Banks or mortgage brokers will assist in your search for the best available rates and terms.

Before you make a decision, if possible speak with a banker with whom you have an established relationship. Compare the banker's terms with those offered by several mortgage brokers.

The Search

1 Find an experienced residential broker through a trusted source. Real estate brokers and agents have access to multiple listing services, which offer more choices in inventory. Your broker will guide you through the process (which can seem tricky at times). Also, start looking into hiring a real estate attorney. You'll want someone lined up and ready to go when you're ready to make an offer.

2 Spend your free time visiting the area where you want to move. See as many houses as you can to educate yourself, price shop, and understand the market by asking your broker for comparables.

3 When looking at a house, ask yourself the following questions:

How long do I plan to live here?

Will this size and configuration accommodate the future needs of my family?

Can I care for a property this size?

Is there adequate parking (driveway, street), storage, appliances, et cetera?

What if I have to resell? Will the house appreciate in value? Suppose I need to sell my house and it doesn't sell for three years? Can I afford the mortgage and maintenance?

4 Get estimates from a contractor for repairs and renovations.

5 Bring someone objective to see the house. You may not notice important things because you are "in love" with it; for example, a nonworking fireplace, a malfunctioning stove, a leaking bathroom, uneven floors.

6 See the house during different times of day (morning, afternoon, night) and on both weekends and weekdays. Check out the surrounding areas for potential problem neighbors. (Is the house across the street from a bar that might be loud at night? A high school?)

7 Be on the lookout for current or potential construction projects. If you think people will be building nearby, know that dirt, noise, and perhaps an obstructed view might be in your future.

8 Knock on neighbors' doors. Talk to them about the neighborhood. Consider going on Facebook and befriending people in the neighborhood who can answer questions you might have about the area.

9 Inspect *everything* (open every door, closet).

10 Ask the current occupant for the past year's utility bills.

11 Get a written comparables report from your broker of every property that was sold in the last three years so you can assess the value of the property.

12 If, after the above, you believe you have found your dream house, place an offer through your real estate broker. The broker and/ or attorney will then guide you through the negotiation process.

The Purchase

Congratulations! Your offer was accepted and you have a binding contract subject to certain contingencies (contracts are usually contingent on loan approval, inspections, and closing date). Now what?

1 Hire a residential real estate attorney (if you haven't already done so) for your closing.

> The closing attorney usually charges a disclosed flat fee, works with your lender, and conducts the necessary title searches

that are part of the due diligence process. This will include checking for liens, tax records, encumbrances, encroachments, easements, et cetera.

As part of the closing, you will purchase title insurance to protect you in the event something is overlooked with conveying a clear title.

You will receive a settlement statement prior to the closing listing all the charges to you (the buyer) as well as those expenses charged to the seller.

2 Conduct inspections.

Hire a professional home inspector as well as a structural engineer to inspect the property. (Brokers, attorneys, and mortgage bankers are all good resources when you're looking for an inspector and structural engineer.) The inspector will check for radon, asbestos, mold, mildew, leaks, malfunctioning appliances and systems, electromagnetic radiation, lead paint, lead in water, and termite damage. A structural engineer will uncover defects that go beyond the scope of the inspector, such as foundation defects. Make sure you fully understand all the potential issues the inspector and engineer come up with prior to executing a contract.

At this juncture you and the seller will decide who will pay for repairs. You may also withdraw your offer if you do not reach a meeting of the minds.

Purchasing a House That Is a New Construction

Do a walk-through with the builder and make a list of everything outstanding that needs to be done before closing. Only deal with reputable builders!

The Closing

• Be prepared. Confirm in advance with your attorney and broker that all necessary inspections have been conducted and that there are no open issues.

• Double-check that you have the proper payments in hand to settle closing fees. You will be informed ahead of time of the amounts to bring to the closing in the form of certified checks. Bring your checkbook for any last-minute changes that might require payments.

• Do a walk-through of the property within twenty-four hours before the closing to make sure there are no last-minute issues. Get the key, alarm codes, and list of vendors who worked on the house. Also make sure all major items (such as appliances) are accounted for.

• Purchase home owner's insurance.

PURCHASING HOME INSURANCE

Factors That Determine Rates

1 House construction: Coastal areas are impacted by hurricanes, winds, and floods. Remember the Three Little Pigs? They knew brick would hold up against that big, bad wolf. You learned that a long time ago. Purchase additional flood insurance from FEMA. This is provided through the National Flood Insurance Program (NFIP). The preliminary insurance usually does not cover the cost of your home and its contents. If you are buying in an earthquake area, remember newer homes are better built because they conform to stricter building codes, or look for older homes that are bolted to their foundations. Earthquake insurance is available in California through the California Earthquake Authority.

2 When was the house built? Wine gets better with age, but older houses become high maintenance. Generally, the older the house, the higher the premium due to special features that are expensive to replicate and compliance with outdated building code.

3 Roof: Insurance companies love new roofs and you should, too. They provide greater protection and fewer problems. Leaks are just not fun. Trust me.

4 Renovations: If you purchase a home in "as is condition," know that you are in store for the ultimate makeover. Premiums will tend to run higher until the renovations and upgrades are completed.

5 Condition of electrical wiring, heating and air-conditioning systems, and plumbing: You get tired after a workout. Well, so do your electrical, heating, and plumbing systems. Have them inspected and upgrade or repair as necessary. Most companies offer maintenance contracts, which I recommend buying from a reputable company.

6 Alarm systems: Smoke, fire, and burglar alarms are like seat belts for your home. You protect your family from dangerous smoke, fire, and intruders. Another green light for a big discount.

7 Pools and wood-burning stoves: These carry huge liability issues. Consider an umbrella policy that equals your net worth. This is so important that I am going to say it again. Get out your yellow highlighter. In the event of a liability on your property, *buy an umbrella policy that equals your net worth.*

8 Fire station: Homes near a professional fire station (as opposed to a volunteer fire department) should receive reduced premiums. It is not necessary that the station employ a Dalmatian.

9 FAIR plans: States offer insurance for high-risk properties where it might be difficult to obtain private insurance. This includes high-crime areas or those areas susceptible to brush fires or hurricanes. Hence the name: Fair Access to Insurance Requirements. These are expensive and may not offer sufficient coverage.

10 Discuss your policy options, deductibles, and discounts with several insurance companies to compare coverage. The higher your deductibles, the lower your premiums will be. Get a reference from a friend.

11 Many states require a seller disclosure form. This will tell you of house ailments you might not normally see. Ask for a house loss history report. This reports any claims filed within the last five years. If these reports reveal any damage, ask about the remedial repairs. You can obtain a C.L.U.E. report from ChoiceTrust or an A-PLUS report from ISO.

12 Inspection Results: A qualified house inspector and a structural engineer will uncover past damage and repairs as well as termite infestation and problems with the plumbing, electrical systems, septic tanks, water heaters, heating, and air-conditioning units. They also check for mold and mildew in the basement, crawl space, and heating ducts as well as determining whether there is an underground oil storage tank. Many insurance companies will not insure homes with these tanks.

Types of Policies to Consider

• Replacement cost: Allows you to rebuild your entire home and replace the furniture and valuables up to the cash value amount listed in the policy. Expensive items must be covered under a separate rider: jewelry, fine art, furs, computers, and musical instruments. You must obtain separate appraisals for each individually listed item. In the event of loss or theft, the deductible is waived.

Extended replacement cost coverage is available for further protection in the event of loss.

- Liability: Obtain the highest possible coverage. Your umbrella coverage will take care of the rest in the event you are sued.

- Guaranteed replacement cost coverage, regardless of cost: Under this coverage, the insurer will pay for everything that was lost or damaged regardless of cost.

- Unlimited building ordinance coverage: This will insure that your rebuilt house will meet the current building codes for fire, electrical, and plumbing.

- Loss of property use: This will pay your costs to live in alternate housing (hotel, rental) while your home is being repaired or rebuilt.

How to Keep Your Costs Down

1 Better credit ratings = lower rates.

2 Get competitive pricing from other agencies.

3 Get a copy of your own loss history report for the prior five years if you have filed any insurance claims in the past.

4 Compare rates for various deductibles. The higher your deductible, the lower your premiums.

5 Bear in mind that discounts are available for multiple policies with one company.

6 Inquire about discounts for:

Fire extinguishers

Indoor sprinkler systems

Burglar and fire alarms that contact an alarm company connected to the police and fire departments

Deadbolt locks and lockable windows

Fire-safe window grates

Owner over the age of fifty

Owner retiree

Owner a longtime policyholder with the same company

Hurricane shutters

Earthquake retrofitting

Significant home upgrades such as new plumbing, heat, air-conditioning units, and new electrical wiring

Smoke detectors

SELLING A HOME TO-DOS

1 Put a FOR SALE sign in front of your house. This is the best way to get your house sold.

Position the sign so it is perpendicular to the house and as close to the street as possible so people can see it. People driving by should be able to easily read the phone numbers on the sign.

Place a light on your sign so people can read it after dark.

2 Locate copies of all of your home improvement bills and keep them in a safe place. You'll need this information to calculate any capital gains.

3 Hire an inspector and fix any problems the inspector says need to be fixed before putting your house on the market. The more items you repair, the fewer problems the buyer's inspector will point out to the potential buyer.

4 Tell your broker about special or interesting features your house offers, such as any improvements you've made and quirky things you love about it, so they can communicate this to prospective buyers.

5 Ask your broker to provide comparable sales in the neighborhood to help you determine a fair asking and selling price. If you don't get an offer within the first month, discuss lowering the price with your broker. Usually the first offer from a qualified buyer will be your best offer.

Information Most Buyers Will Want to Know

• Construction details: A description of unique construction or design details

• Home history (When was the house built? How old is the roof?)

• Market analysis: Make sure your real estate broker has a copy of your competitive market analysis (comparables).

- Neighborhood profile: Information on local stores, services, places of worship, schools, transportation, parks, and so on

- Personal info: When you bought the house, reason for selling, is there anything you would be willing to sell with the house, what is not staying in the house, what price you are ready to sell the house for

- Selling incentives: What makes your house great? Any special history about the house?

- Utilities: Have a copy of your utility bills from the past year.

Preparing Your Home for Showings

Banish Odors

1 Bake something like cookies or an apple pie if you want your house to smell homey (or need to mask an un-homey scent).

2 Rid your house of the smell of cigarette, cigar, or pipe smoke. The smell of smoke has killed many deals.

General Cleanliness

1 Clean the windows and window screens. You want the potential buyer to be able to see out the windows.

2 Dust the furniture.

3 Empty all garbage cans.

4 Your kitchen, in particular, should be spotless. Do not leave any dishes in the sink.

5 Make the beds.

6 Put away any extra items that clutter the house.

7 Vacuum all carpets.

Outdoor Spruce Ups

1 Mow your lawn and clean up the grounds in general.

2 Green is good: Plant flowers.

Miscellaneous

1 Fresh flowers always make a house look beautiful. Put some in vases around your home.

2 Get your pet out of the house.

3 If you can, make yourselves scarce. Potential buyers do not want to meet current owners.

4 Light a fire in the fireplace.

5 Move cars so the potential buyers can park easily.

6 Open the doors to all rooms (do not try to hide a space, no matter how small or out of the way it is).

7 Put away personal pictures. Potential buyers do not want to see the "life" of the family living there. They want to be able to imagine themselves living there.

8 Put away valuables. Unfortunately, sometimes people steal jewelry and other easy-to-grab items.

9 Replace lightbulbs. Use bulbs that cast a flattering light and emphasize true colors.

10 Set the temperature (it should not be too cold or too hot).

11 Turn on all the lights in the house.

12 Play classical music on the stereo.

13 Put out bottled water and—if you feel inclined—cookies for potential buyers to enjoy as they walk through. The more comfortable they feel in your house, the more likely they are to buy it!

MOVING CHECKLIST

Two Months Before the Move

Miscellaneous To-Dos

1 Arrange to take time off from your job.

2 If you have kids, get them involved with the move so it will be fun for them. Have them help pack the boxes and label them with stickers.

3 Call friends and family for moving company recommendations.

4 Contact several moving companies for estimates. Look for:

> Companies willing to do an advance walk-through of your space prior to the move date to gauge time, number of trips, manpower, and other unexpected issues.

> Sufficient theft, injury, damage, and loss insurance.

> Companies that are bonded and security cleared.

> Companies that will sign a written contract.

5 Arrange a new layout for furniture in your new home (you can do this at the website www.plan3d.com by drawing a plan of all the rooms in your new house, numbering each room). Try to figure out:

Which pieces you are taking, placing in storage, or giving away. If storage is necessary, start thinking about where you will rent a storage unit.

What furniture and accessories you will need to buy.

Print out three copies of your furniture plan. Keep one copy, store one copy in a safe place, and share one copy with the leader of the move team on the day of the move.

6 Make all travel arrangements (hotel, flights, car rental, et cetera) for your family for moving day well in advance.

7 Start keeping all receipts for moving-related expenses in a designated moving folder. Some moving expenses may be tax deductible (you will need to download and print IRS Form 8822 and Form 3903 to file).

8 Contact your insurance agent to discuss transferring existing medical, property, fire, and auto insurance and to insure the move and the new house (keep insurance on your old house until the new owners move in).

Current Residence To-Dos

1 Appraisals: Make sure antique, art, and jewelry appraisals are current before the move.

2 Notify your current utility companies—gas, phone, electric, water, cable TV—of disconnect dates (the day you leave) in advance and your forwarding address for a final bill. (Or your Realtor can arrange for a transfer of services to the new owner, which involves no disconnects.) If you have "last month" deposits with services, such as the telephone, water, gas, and electric companies, request your refund and give them your new address to send the check.

3 Important documents: Gather all important documents, such as copies of wills and birth certificates, passports, or important personal items such as jewelry and medications, and keep them in a safe place. You will want to carry these items yourself to your new home.

New Residence To-Dos

1 Ask the previous owners for blueprints of the home and get several sets made. You never know when you'll need them.

2 If you're moving into an apartment or condo, contact your super to reserve the freight elevator and a parking space for the moving van. Some buildings have specific dates and times when the freight elevator is available. Call well in advance.

3 Buy home owner's insurance for your new home.

4 Ask the current owners of your new home if they were happy with the following service providers (if applicable), and if so, get the contact info for:

      Electrician

      Landscaper

      Plumber

      Pool service

5 Speak to the current owners about any work that might need to be done on the following and arrange to have it repaired or installed before you move in:

      Electrical wiring

      Emergency generator

      Fire alarm and protection system

      Kitchen equipment

      New carpets and curtains

      Paint, woodwork

HOME

Plumbing

Satellite dish, cable TV

Security alarm

Septic tank or well

Technology needs (e.g., wireless internet, high-speed internet, and so on)

Water softener and water purification systems

6 Decide if you need to find new contacts for the following:

Bank

Doctors

Drugstore

Dry cleaner

Grocery store

Gym

Hospital

Movie theater

Place of worship

Post office

Shoemaker

Shopping center

Sitters and housekeeper

Transportation

One Month Before the Move

1 Begin packing (if you are packing yourself). Start with items that you will not need immediately, such as out-of-season clothes.

2 Go to the post office and fill out a change of address form. In addition, give your new address to:

> Banks and financial institutions
>
> Credit card companies
>
> Friends and family members
>
> Health care providers (doctors, pharmacists)
>
> Insurance companies
>
> Local government agencies, federal agencies, the IRS
>
> Magazines and newspapers
>
> Schools
>
> Utility companies

3 Notify the moving company if there are any changes in the dates of your move.

4 Make a note of anything that is being repaired or cleaned, so you don't forget it.

5 Car servicing: If you are driving a long distance to your new residence, have your car serviced a week or two prior to moving day.

Two Weeks Before Moving

1 Transfer bank accounts to your new bank. Empty your safe deposit box at the old bank and put the contents in a box at the new one.

2 Back up all your computer files. Consider taking all backup files with you personally in the event your computer equipment gets damaged in the move.

3 Transfer all prescriptions to a drugstore in your new location. Have an adequate supply of medications during the move. Be aware that some prescriptions cannot be transferred and some types of medications (e.g., your child's medication for AD/HD) require a doctor's prescription to refill.

4 Cancel newspaper service.

5 Contact the alarm company to determine who will be the emergency contact person and get the new alarm code.

6 Make final packing decisions on what you are taking and what you are not. This is the time to make arrangements for what you want to put in storage or give away.

7 Contact your new utility companies to tell them when to begin service.

8 Drain all the oil and gas from your power equipment so it will be moved safely.

9 Hire someone to clean your new home prior to moving in. (It's much easier to clean *before* the furniture is in place.)

10 If you are living in a rental, make any necessary repairs to ensure the return of your security deposit.

11 Begin to pack the luggage that you will personally take with you. These items include:

> Cell phone, BlackBerry or PDA, laptop
>
> Eyeglasses (buy a spare or two)
>
> First-aid kit and toiletries
>
> Games and entertainment for the children
>
> Important documents (birth certificates, passports, wills, et cetera)
>
> Medications

12 Use up inventory: Start using foods and cleaning supplies that cannot be moved. Try not to move cleaning supplies and other materials that can pose a danger or cause damage if they leak or spill.

Out-of-State Moves: Additional To-Dos

1. Select a new bank, establish accounts and get a safe deposit box.

2. Go to the DMV for new license plates, new driver's license, and new registration of your cars.

3. Gather personal records from doctors, lawyers, accountants, and schools.

→

4. Enroll the kids in a new school and arrange for the transfer of their school records.

5. Obtain names, phone numbers, and requirements (such as deposits) for utility companies.

One Week Before Moving

1 Mark which items you'll take yourself, so the movers won't load them on the van.

2 Number each box and make a list of the contents in each box. This list will be critical when you are unloading into your new home. Label the room the box is destined for.

3 Mark your boxes to be shipped with labels like "Fragile," "This Side Up," "Do Not Load," and "Load Last."

4 Finish packing your personal suitcases.

5 Finalize all travel arrangements for your family.

6 Settle any bills with local businesses.

7 Schedule a "move out" garbage pickup for large items.

8 Get certified checks for the amounts listed in your moving contract. Have cash for tipping the movers.

One Day Before Moving

1 Disconnect all major appliances for the move, such as refrigerators, ovens, et cetera.

2 Print out at least four copies of your final list of boxes and their contents, your furniture layout plan, and any last-minute notes.

3 Pack a box of things you'll need as soon as you arrive at your new home. Take this box with you or have the movers load it last and unload it first. Clearly mark this box "Load Last."

4 Double-check to make sure all items traveling in your car—such as your medications and your children's favorite toys—are in an out-of-the-way location so they will not be loaded on the truck.

5 Packing up your plants: Plants do not travel well, so you may want to think about donating them to a hospital, temple, or church.

6 Arrive at your home a day ahead of time, if possible, to make sure utilities are connected and to plan placement of major items in your home.

Moving Day To-Dos

1 Be on hand when the driver arrives and throughout the loading process. If you won't be there, make sure someone will be present to direct the movers. Give the foreman—usually the driver—the name and phone number of the person handling your move.

HOME

2 Check on the condition of your furniture and special items as they are loaded onto the truck.

3 Do a final walk-through of your home to make sure nothing was missed.

4 Sign the bill of lading and make sure your new address and phone number are listed correctly.

5 Lock all windows and doors, and turn off all electrical switches.

Move-In Day To-Dos

1 Before the movers arrive:

Have plastic sheeting put down in all major walkways and rooms so the movers don't track in dirt or damage carpets or flooring.

Have food and drinks ready for you, your family, and your movers while boxes are being unloaded.

Place Post-its and French chalk on floors and walls to mark positions for the furniture.

Take doors off hinges, if necessary. Make sure paths are clear.

2 Pay the foreman with cash, traveler's check, certified check, or money order prior to your goods being unloaded.

3 Check your belongings carefully and note any damaged items on the inventory paperwork.

4 Supervise unloading and unpacking.

5 Stand at the front door and mark your master list for each box or item unloaded (your boxes should be numbered and marked with the room destination).

6 Call the locksmith to change locks.

7 Arrange to have someone connect electrical and gas appliances.

8 Check for any damage to the walls, floors, woodwork, molding, or doors that may have occurred during unloading.

9 When you determine all is okay, sign the mover's paperwork and tip the foreman.

New Home To-Dos After Move In

1 Run all water, turn on all lights. Make a list of what works and what doesn't.

2 Have a practice fire drill and form an evacuation plan with your family, so they know how to handle an emergency in the new house. Review where to go and what to do in case of a tornado, hurricane, flood, blackout, or other emergency. See pages 233–54 for emergency plans.

3 Place flashlights around the house.

4 Childproof your home if necessary.

5 Test security and smoke alarms, check fire extinguishers.

6 Make a list of all local emergency numbers (for an example, see pages 68–72) and post it in an easily accessible place near a phone.

7 Compile all receipts from the move and file them for tax purposes.

8 Send in claims for damages sustained during the move.

9 Introduce yourself to your new neighbors.

10 Celebrate!

CONGRATULATIONS! YOU ARE NOW A HOMEOWNER!

Keep Your Insurance Policy Up to Date

1 Photograph the contents of your home and inventory valuables such as paintings, art, jewelry, and furs at least once a year.

2 Keep your insurance coverage up to date with the repairs and renovations to your property.

3 Keep your policies, appraisals, and inventories in a safe place. Keep a scanned backup copy on your computer.

4 Maintain your house to the best of your ability (just as you would your car). Be sure to let your insurance company know if you have done any major improvements or renovations to the house.

5 Major purchases as well as marriage or divorce will change your insurance needs. Contact your broker if you need to update your policy for any reason.

6 If you are not satisfied with the service or prices you have with your current broker, discuss those concerns or do comparison shopping.

HOUSEHOLD BUDGET

Before setting your household budget, it's a good idea to fill out a family financial profile. That will show you exactly where you stand before you start determining how much you can spend, and it ensures that you'll have all of this important information compiled in one place.

Family Profile

List the following information for each member of the family.

PERSONAL INFORMATION

Social Security number

Date of birth

Place of birth

Mother's maiden name

Passport number and expiration date

Driver's license number and expiration date

Frequent flyer numbers (all airlines)

CREDIT CARDS

List all credit cards

Account numbers

Cardholders

Names on the card

Maiden name

Expiration dates

Credit card 800 numbers

User names

Passwords

Websites

Secret answers

Online account user IDs

Customer service email addresses

BANK ACCOUNTS

Name of bank

Account number

Purpose of account (checking, savings)

Account manager

Contact info (telephone number, email, website)

User name

Password

Security questions

PROPERTIES AND MORTGAGE PAYMENTS

HOME

Property

Value

Use

Financing

Bank

Payment method

Loan amount

Interest rate

Loan maturity

Loan type

Account

Website

User name

Password

Security questions

Email for communication alerts

VENDOR INFO

Service

User

Account number

Payment method

Website

User name

Password

Security code

Email for communication alerts

Amount (if recurring fixed payment)

Other

INSURANCE (ALL TYPES)

Carrier

Insured

Type of policy coverage

Account number

Policy number

Expiration date

Contact person

Phone number

Annual premium

Website

Policy Benefit

Beneficiary

Payer

User name

Password

Creating Your Household Budget

Now you're ready to determine your family's budget. Purchase household budget and bill-paying software to facilitate your budget process, then gather the following information:

Monthly net income: _____

Monthly expenses: _____

Rent or mortgage: _____

UTILITIES

Gas

Electric

Water

House phone

Cell phone

Cable, dish, modem

Other

LOANS

Car

Student

Other

INSURANCE

    House

    Health

    Car

    Savings

    Disability

    Professional liability

    Mortgage

    Other

HOME

CHARITABLE DONATIONS

OTHER

    Pet expenses

    Restaurants

    Clothes

    Gifts

    Vacations

    Food, groceries

    Cleaners

    Cars and gasoline

    Auto maintenance

    Employees (housekeepers, babysitters)

    Employment taxes for employees

School expenses

Miscellaneous

Total Expenses: _____

Net Income: _____

MUST-HAVE CONTACT INFORMATION

Compile this information and post it in an easily accessible place.

Home Contact List of Vendors

	NAME	CONTACT INFO
Air-conditioning		
Alarm company		
Appliance repair		
Audio/video repair		
Auto body shop		
Bicycle shop		
Cable TV or satellite		
Carpenter		
Carpet cleaner		
Chimney cleaner		
Curtain repair		
Electric company		

	NAME	CONTACT INFO
Electrician		
Exterminator		
Firewood supply		
Framer		
Garbage removal		
Gas company		
Glass and mirror		
Hardware store		
Housekeeper		
Landscaper		
Locksmith		
Marble and tile repair		
Mover		
Newspaper delivery		
Nursery for plants		

HOME

	NAME	CONTACT INFO
Painter		
Piano service		
Plumber		
Pool service		
Power authority		
Roof and gutter maintenance		
Sprinkler		
Storage unit		
Tech support		
Telephone company		
Water delivery		
Wildlife rescue		
Window washers		

General Household Contact List

Brother/sister		
Church/ synagogue		
Doctor (adults)		
Doctor (children)		
Dry cleaner		
Emergency: Who to call		
Father		
FedEx/UPS		
Florist		
Garage		
Gym		
Hairdresser		
Hospital		
Liquor store		
Mother		
Movie theater		

	NAME	CONTACT INFO
Neighbors		
Office/work		
Pharmacy		
Pizza delivery		
Post office		
Shoemaker		
Taxi		

TOOLBOX: WHAT EVERYONE SHOULD OWN

Bar clamp

Combination square

Combination wrench set

Cordless drill (12 volt)

Drill bit set (high-speed steel)

Dust mask; try to find a heavy-duty one

Epoxy (Duro Master Mend)

Extension cord

File set (5-piece)

Flashlight

Glue (Elmer's Glue-All)

Glue gun

Glue sticks

Hammer (13 oz.)

Hobby pliers set

Instant Krazy Glue

Level

L-handle hex key set

Locking pliers

Lubricant (WD-40)

Masking tape

Masonry drill bit

Nails

Packaging tape

Pliers/adjustable wrench set

Pry bar

Putty knife

Safety glasses

Safety step

Sandpaper

Saw nest (get one with a plastic handle)

Scratch awl

Screwdriver bit set

Screwdriver set

Screws

Snap knife

Socket and wrench set

Staple gun tacker

Staples

Tape measure (25 ft.)

Tote bag

Women's pigskin leather palm gloves

Wood boring drill bit set

YEARLY HOUSEHOLD MAINTENANCE CHECKLIST

If possible, try to do the following a few times each year. Even if you can only do some of them once every year, your home will benefit greatly!

1 Air-conditioning: Evaporative A/C: Replace blankets, check air flow, clean or repair unit. Refrigerated A/C: Clean or replace filter; clean condenser, evaporator coils, and condensation drain.

2 Appliances: Clean the clothes dryer exhaust duct, damper, and space under the dryer; clean the kitchen exhaust hood and air filters; check the water hoses on the clothes washer, refrigerator, ice maker, water heater, and dishwasher for cracks and bubbles.

3 Basement, foundation: Check for cracks and moisture; repair if necessary.

4 Bathroom and kitchen tile: Clean and wax.

5 Carpets, curtains: Professionally clean.

6 Clothes dryer: Change filter and vacuum lint from ducts and surrounding areas.

7 Clothes washer: Clean water inlet filters; check hoses for leaks and replace if necessary.

8 Drain, waste, and vent systems: Flush out.

9 Electrical system: Check to make sure that extension cords are not overloaded and are safely located.

10 Exhaust fan: Clean grill and fan blades.

11 Exterior: Check the safety condition of outdoor areas. Look for rot, check for stability, treat annually with water sealant; install motion-sensitive lights at the front and back entrances of the home.

12 Fire extinguishers: Make sure they are accessible; check to see if they're fully charged; make sure the expiration dates are not within the next year.

13 Fireplace: Have chimney cleaned and inspected; make sure damper is functioning properly; confirm that fire extinguisher is located nearby.

14 Floor drain strainer: Clean out debris and scrub strainer.

15 Frozen pipe prevention: Insulate exposed pipes in crawl spaces, basement, and attic.

16 Garage doors: Clean and lubricate hinges, rollers, and tracks; tighten screws.

17 Garbage disposal: Flush with hot water and baking soda; put ice cubes through to sharpen blades.

18 Gas burner: Clean burners and ports.

19 Generator: Test to see if it's working properly.

20 Gutters and downspout: Clean out, inspect, and repair weaknesses; check for proper drainage and adjust if necessary.

21 Heating system: Have furnace cleaned and checked; change filters; make sure nothing is stored near furnace or hot water heater. Hot water heating system: Test relief valve and replace if necessary; check pressure gauge and drain expansion tank if necessary. Forced air heating system: Clean or replace air filter and vacuum registers; clean and lubricate blower blades and motor; check fan belt tension and adjust if necessary; replace cracked or worn belt; check for leaks in ducts; repair as necessary.

22 Heating pump: Clean or replace air filter; clean condenser, evaporator coils, and condensation drain; remove snow and/or debris from outdoor portion of unit; lubricate blower motor.

23 Kitchen: Take everything off every shelf and scrub down the entire room.

24 Mattresses: Flip, rotate.

25 Oil burner: Inspect and clean.

26 Pest control: If necessary, exterminate in any problem areas.

27 Plumbing: Inspect the shutoff valves at each plumbing fixture to make sure they function properly; repair loose or missing grout or caulking in tub/shower to prevent deterioration of tiles.

28 Refrigerator: Wash and check door gasket; vacuum condenser coils.

29 Roof: Check condition; inspect surface, flashing, eaves, and soffits and repair if necessary; clean gutters to prevent leaks.

30 Security alarm: Test system. Make sure security features linked to door fixtures are working properly.

31 Septic tank: Have a professional check the tank (watch for backup throughout the year).

32 Sink and tub: Clean out debris in drains; soak stoppers in vinegar and water.

33 Smoke alarms: Check batteries and replace as necessary.

34 Thermostat: Clean heat sensor, contact points, and contacts; check accuracy; replace if necessary.

35 Toilet: Check for leaks in flushing mechanism; repair if necessary.

36 Upholstery: Dry-clean.

37 Water heater: Drain water until clear to eliminate sediment; inspect flue assembly and clean burner ports (for gas heater); test temperature pressure relief valve and replace if necessary.

38 Window and door weather stripping: Inspect and repair; if deteriorating, replace.

39 Windows: Wash.

Special Considerations for Specific Months

March: Note how daylight savings time might affect your time zone and change clocks accordingly.

April: Turn on air-conditioning compressor. Install window screens for summer.

October: Note how daylight savings time might affect your time zone and change clocks accordingly.

November: Remove window screens.

CLEANING CHECKLIST

> **Note:** Make your own list of requirements of what you want done specifically for each room.

Weekly

Bathrooms

1 Scour shower and/or bathtub.

2 Scrub toilets.

3 Clean sink.

4 Clean windows.

5 Empty trash cans.

6 Clean mirrors.

7 Vacuum and mop floors.

8 Replenish towels, tissues, and toilet paper as needed.

9 Check toiletries and replenish as needed.

10 Check laundry basket and do laundry as needed.

Bedrooms

1 Change sheets and other bedding.

2 Dust shelves and organize contents.

3 Dust all surfaces.

4 Vacuum rugs (remember to vacuum under bed and furniture) and wash floors (if not carpeted).

5 Open windows to air out room (weather permitting).

Kitchen

1 Throw away any foods that could go bad in the refrigerator and clean it inside and out. Clean sink and pour boiling water down drain.

2 Wipe out insides of microwave and oven.

3 Clean small electrical devices (coffee maker, tea kettle, toaster, et cetera).

4 Empty trash can and recycling bin.

5 Vacuum and mop floors.

Living Room, Dining Room, Family Room

1 Wipe fingerprints off doors and woodwork.

2 Dust.

3 Fluff sofa cushions.

4 Vacuum floors and/or rugs and carpets.

5 Wash floors (if not carpeted).

MISCELLANEOUS

Wipe handprints from all doors and woodwork.

Sweep garage.

Recycle or throw away unwanted magazines and newspapers.

Vacuum vents.

Wipe down outdoor furniture.

Water all plants and change water in flower arrangements.

Wipe all telephones (this is where germs live).

Wash down outside areas (terrace, sidewalks).

Clean outdoor garbage containers.

Water outdoor plants.

Seasonally

Bathrooms

1 Scrub grout (do this monthly, if possible).

2 Wash shower curtain.

3 Check expiration dates on all medications (over-the-counter and prescription).

Bedrooms

1 Refresh linens: Wash duvet covers, pillow protectors, mattress pads, shams (do this monthly, if possible).

2 Turn and flip over mattresses.

3 Launder or dry-clean blankets.

Kitchen

1 Check freezer for items that should be thrown away. Clean and deodorize.

2 Wipe ceiling.

3 Organize pantry and throw out old food (do this monthly, if possible).

4 Wash stove vents.

Living Room

1 Vacuum fireplace screens.

2 Fireplace: Clean out and have a professional clean the flue.

3 Flip sofa cushions (do this monthly, if possible).

Entire House

1 Wipe down interior and exterior doors.

2 Flush drains with vinegar, boiling water, and baking soda.

3 Vacuum window treatments, moldings, windowsills.

Every Spring

1 Take all books off shelves and dust thoroughly.

2 Professionally clean carpets, upholstery, and window treatments.

3 Oil window and door hinges.

4 Dust radiators.

5 Reseal stone and grout.

6 Remove, wash, and store storm windows.

7 Wash windows and affix window screens for summer use.

8 Wax wood floors and furniture.

9 Clean gutters, outdoor furniture, and utility spaces.

HOUSEKEEPERS

Interview Questionnaire

HOME

1 What do you consider to be your daily responsibilities? Cooking, cleaning, babysitting?

2 What cleaning products do you use?

3 What was a typical day like at your previous employer's?

4 Were you responsible for cooking? If yes, what would you typically cook?

5 Did the family have kids? If yes, how did that impact your responsibilities?

6 Did you ever oversee any repairmen in the house? If yes, what was the last situation you had to take care of?

7 Can you sew on a button?

8 How do you communicate with your employers?

9 Why do you want to leave your current employer?

10 Do they know you want to leave?

11 What do you like best about your job? What do you like least?

12 What are you currently earning?

13 How long have you worked in your current position?

14 Do you smoke? How often?

15 Do you drink? How often?

16 Do you take any medication, or have any allergies that would affect your ability to do your job?

17 Do you drive? If so, how often do you drive? Do you feel comfortable driving on the highway?

18 How will you get to work?

19 Do you have any responsibilities or commitments that would prevent you from staying late or working on weekends?

20 Do you mind getting a health examination before starting work?

Questions for References

1 How long did she work for you?

2 Why did she leave?

3 What were her responsibilities?

4 What did you pay her?

5 Would you hire her again?

6 If you had to name three negative qualities about her, what would they be?

7 Did you ever suspect she was drinking on the job? Abusing drugs? Had an eating disorder? Legal or financial trouble?

8 Was she reliable? Please give a few examples.

9 How often did she miss work?

WHAT TO HAVE IN YOUR KITCHEN

POTS AND PANS

12-quart stockpot with lid

2-quart stockpot with lid

1-quart stockpot with lid

10-inch frying pan with lid

2 casseroles with lids

2 saucepans with lids

Cake pan

Pie pan

Bread pan

APPLIANCES

Stand mixer with 5-quart bowl

Food processor

Blender

Coffee maker

Hand mixer

Microwave

Toaster/toaster oven

UTENSILS

15-inch stainless steel bowl

Baking sheets

Box grater

Colander

Cooling rack

Cutting board

Fine strainer

Freeze, heat, and serve dishes

Glass baking dishes

Instant response thermometer

Knives: paring, serrated, carving

Measuring cups

Measuring spoons

Pepper mill

Plastic pouring spouts

Salad spinner

Spatula

Steamer basket

Stovetop grill

Tea kettle

Timer

Tongs

Whisk

Wooden spoon

RESOURCES

BOOKS

Be My Guest, by Rena Kirdar Sindi

The Comfort Table, by Katie Lee Joel

Entertaining, by Martha Stewart

Fête Accompli!, by Lara Shriftman, Elizabeth Harrison, and Karen Robinovitz

InStyle Parties, by the Editors of *InStyle*

Joy of Cooking, by Irma S. Rombauer, Marion Rombauer Becker, and Ethan Becker

Martha Stewart's Homekeeping Handbook, by Martha Stewart

Silver Palate Cookbook, by Julee Rosso and Sheila Lukins

365, by Rachael Ray

MAGAZINES

Better Homes and Gardens

Dwell

Elle Decor

Good Housekeeping

Martha Stewart Living

O, The Oprah Magazine

Real Simple

Time Style & Design

STORES FOR HOME FURNISHING STAPLES

There are tons of home goods stores, but the following will help you get started setting up your home sweet home:

- Amazon.com: A good place to find deals on appliances

- Bed, Bath & Beyond: bedbathandbeyond.com

- The Container Store: containerstore.com

- Furniture/home sections of department stores: Retailers periodically put inventory on sale, and you can get amazing deals both in strore and online.

- Ikea: ikea.com

- Target: target.com

And these places offer products that will help make your house feel like a home:

- Anthropologie: anthropologie.com

- Crate & Barrel: crateandbarrel.com

- eBay.com: Excellent for finding quirky collectibles

- Pottery Barn: potterybarn.com

- Williams-Sonoma: williams-sonoma.com

PREGNANCY

Congratulations! The line on the stick has just turned blue and your world will never be the same! Pregnancy brings a whole new set of joys, worries, and things to plan and do. It's amazing to think that at one point, the only choices facing mothers was whether or not to give birth in the field or by the stove in the kitchen, depending on the season. Nowadays it is easy to become overwhelmed by the choices we have, but by preparing well in advance of your due date (you never know), your birthing experience and first weeks at home can be comfortable and relatively stress-free.

Did you know that hospital linens rival government-issue bedding for comfort? Bring your own favorite, brightly colored pillowcase (so the hospital staff doesn't lose it in the wash) to get you through the few days you may spend there.

Do you like cabbage? You will if your breasts become engorged after giving birth! Even if you have never cooked a cruciferous vegetable in your life, placing the refrigerated cabbage leaves over your breasts will help reduce the swelling. Don't ask me how. It just works. (And no, it doesn't smell great, but you won't care.)

Through personal experience and "scientific

research" (i.e., polling every single one of my girlfriends who have given birth), I have come up with the ne plus ultra of what you will need, what you will *not* need, and what you can expect from hospital to homecoming.

IMMEDIATE TO-DOS

1 Go to the doctor. She'll give you the most important to-dos!

2 Start reading pregnancy books and magazines (see page 117 for suggested reading).

3 Decide when you are going to share your news and with whom. Make sure your partner is on board with the plan.

4 Begin investigating the type of delivery you want to have (labor assistant, doula, midwife).

SECOND TRIMESTER TO-DOS

Take time during your nine months of pregnancy to do the following. It'll be worth it!

1 Take *lots* of photos while you are pregnant. I wish I had taken more when I was really big. I know being photographed feels like the last thing in the world you want to do, but you will wish you had. I even went to a professional photographer and had beautiful black-and-white photos taken of myself and my husband, and I love them.

2 Go shopping! Start stocking up on all of the items you'll need once the baby arrives (see page 96 through 110 for lists of specific items).

3 Start your babysitter/nanny search. Call all your friends and family and tell them you are looking for a babysitter or nanny (if you need one). The search can never start too early.

4 Install nanny cams. If you're planning on installing cameras, the time to do this would be before you hire a nanny, while you are pregnant. I had nanny cams installed. Fortunately, nothing bad was ever caught on tape, but I strongly recommend installing cameras ahead of time if you plan to do it at all, because you will be super overwhelmed after you have the baby.

5 Visit the hospital you are going to give birth in to see if you will be comfortable with it. If you are not, then you want to have plenty of time to find a new hospital (which might result in having to find a new doctor) or perhaps even considering a home birth like I did!

6 Think about cord blood banking and look into options if applicable (www.viacord.com and www.cbr.com).

7 Find a pediatrician and make arrangements, so they will give your child their first exam at the hospital.

8 Sign up for baby registries.

THIRD TRIMESTER TO-DOS

1 Find a lactation consultant. Before I gave birth the first time, I didn't realize how hard it is to breast-feed. If you are serious about it and think it is something you want to do, I strongly suggest you see a lactation consultant in the hospital or before. It seems like something that would come naturally, but for many mothers it does not. And if you don't see someone within the first week of giving birth, your milk could dry up.

2 Clean all baby furniture, clothing, and items that are new or have been in storage before setting them up for your new baby. Put new batteries in your baby monitor and any other electronic devices you'll need.

3 Buy one nursing bra predelivery and then wait to see what size you are once you give birth, and buy more then. People always expect you to be bigger than you actually are, and these bras are expensive.

ONE MONTH BEFORE DELIVERY TO-DOS

1 Pack. You never know, you might go into labor early (see hospital packing list on page 110).

2 Create a list of people who should receive a birth announcement. Make sure their addresses are up to date.

3 Choose your stationery (birth announcement and thank-you cards). Or consider sending an email announcement. It's more efficient and modern!

4 Buy stamps. You will need these for all those thank-you cards.

5 Address birth announcement envelopes. Prepare the email you will send people from the hospital. Discuss with your partner the language of the message and the recipient list.

6 Install the baby's car seat. The hospital won't let you go home unless you have a car seat installed properly in your car.

7 Apply lanolin to your nipples at least one week before your due date if you're planning to breast-feed. Use a Q-tip so it doesn't get all over your fingers. It is hard to wash off.

8 Ask someone to come visit you in the hospital (i.e., friend or parent) who can bring breakfast the day after you give birth. Those bagels will be greatly appreciated!

9 Assign someone in your family to buy a newspaper on the day your child is born. It's a great piece of memorabilia for you and your child.

10 Make an emergency contact list. This is not the same list you will make for the hospital. This is a list of emergency contacts for your future babysitter. You may be thinking, why make it now? Well, when you finally decide to get out of the house, you might be so excited that you are finally getting a break, you'll leave without remembering to make it. Make sure you include the phone numbers of your pediatrician, the address of the closest hospital, the poison control number, the phone number of the nearest twenty-four-hour pharmacy, and contact information for any other person you might want the sitter to call. Give them a copy and have one copy taped near each telephone.

11 Make a mix CD or an iPod playlist of music for your delivery. If you create a CD, make extra copies, as these can make good thank-you gifts to people who were especially helpful during your pregnancy.

12 Sterilize and organize baby bottles.

13 Make sure your gas tank is always at least half full.

14 Purchase your baby pharmacy items (see page 104).

WHAT TO BUY

Nursery Must-Haves

• Air purifier

• Alcohol (for cleaning the belly button)

• Baby calendar: Buy one before you are due. You will want to take time to write down all the baby's "firsts" and will never think to buy it once the baby is born.

• Baby monitor: For the first year, you will want a digital monitor so that you can see your baby throughout the night.

• Baby thermometer (digital)

• Bathtub: The first few weeks you will be bathing baby on a counter or on the changing table using a plastic bowl, maybe even in the kitchen sink. Then you'll move to a plastic bath that sits in the tub once the baby is close to one year old.

• Blankets

- Bottled water (it's very important to drink a lot of water if you are breast feeding)

- Burp cloths: Buy and wash a ton and have them ready in advance.

- CD player/iPod: Sounds and songs can soothe the baby (and you!), so I recommend having a CD player or iPod dock in the nursery.

- Clock: You will need digital clocks everywhere since you will be keeping a very close record of everything your baby does.

- Diaper pail: Get a simple diaper pail with a tight-fitting lid.

- Humidifier

- Infants' Tylenol

- Keepsake box: Find a pretty place to keep the newspaper from the baby's day of birth, as well as baby's hospital wristband, first hat, et cetera.

- Mobile: Since babies cannot see color for the first few months, buy a black-and-white mobile—your baby will respond right away.

- Night-lights/flashlights: You will want flash-lights everywhere. You'll be up at all kinds of crazy hours, and turning on overhead lights can be jarring. Plastic Candela lights are great, too— you can position them all over the nursery. Small reading lights are handy.

- Pedialyte (in case the baby throws up or has diarrhea)

- Refrigerator and bottle warmer: If possible, have a small fridge in the nursery for formula and bottled water and a bottle warmer for heating the formula during nighttime feedings.

- Sleeping and feeding journal. Your doctor will ask you for all this information at checkups.

- Tissues

Furniture

- Crib: There are so many kinds. Be sure to try to put the bed rail down in the store and see if you find it easy to work. Also, make sure you can lower the mattress as baby grows.

- Crib mattress: Get one that has a high safety rating and is appropriate for a toddler on one side, infant on the other.

- Rocking chair and stool ("glider"): You will spend so much time in this, it's worth spending money on a comfortable one.

- Changing table: Make sure you get one large enough to store all the items you will need to keep handy, like diapers and wipes. (See page 106 for a full list of items.) Also be sure it has a safety belt.

- Changing table cushion and terry cloth pad: Get a contoured one.

Gear

- BabyBjörn carrier/sling: This is the most awesome thing. It's the most comfortable way to carry your child; you won't want to go anywhere without it. However, don't remove tags till baby is born. Some babies love them, some babies don't.

• Bouncy seat: This is a must. Your child will live in this.

• Car seat: Get one of these and install it early. You will need one for infant, one for six-to-twelve month-old, then a forward-facing one for when the baby is bigger. Some seats can face either way and therefore eliminate the need for the intermediate seat.

• Portable crib and playpen

• Play mat: I couldn't live without a portable play/rest area.

• Swing

• Strollers: You will probably end up buying multiple strollers since you will need different strollers for different stages. I suggest:

  • Stage 1: I recommend finding a stroller and car seat in one, preferably with a large basket. This type of stroller will last up to six months.

  • Stage 2: I recommend getting a stroller on which you can flip the handle back and forth. On some, while the baby is still not totally sitting up, you can stroll them facing backward, a feature I liked.

    You may need an umbrella stroller, too. This will be your final stroller purchase. Get the lightest one possible and make sure it is easy to collapse but steady when locked to go.

Linens

- Bedding: Almost every baby store has a good selection of bedding. Get a couple of extra crib sheets in addition to the ones that come with your set. Make sure they fit *very* tightly, per safety recommendations, and don't put pillows or fluffy items in the crib with the baby.

- Towels: Get at least five large ones with hoods, and ten washcloths.

- Waterproof mattress pads (2).

Bottle-Feeding Supplies

- Formula: Ask your pediatrician what brand they prefer. Even if you're planning on breast-feeding, make sure you have some on hand *just in case*.

- Bottles: There are millions of different bottles, but the main thing to make sure of is that they are bisphenol A (BPA) free. BPA is a chemical found in some plastics that recent reports suggest may be harmful to a baby's health.

- Bottle sterilizer: You can buy bottle sterilizer machines or you can sterilize in a pot of boiling water.

- Dishwashing liquid soap to clean bottles

- Bottle dryer rack

- Bottle brush: Get the one that goes with the type of bottles you buy.

- Bottle accessories holder for dishwasher

- Bottle tote: Get an insulated one.

- Bottle warmer

- Nipples: Every baby is different when it comes to nipples, so it'll be a bit of a trial and error period at first. Bear in mind that there are different levels of nipples. You need a slow flow when they are young, and then you will increase the flow as they get older.

- Bibs: Cuteness is important, but be sure to get bibs that are easy to clean. Buy 8.

- Burp cloths: Buy these prefolded. You can never have enough of them. I recommend buying 24.

Breast-feeding Supplies

- You'll want a couple of good books on the subject and a lactation consultant's number for middle-of-the-night questions.

- A boppy baby nursing pillow, or similar pillow is nice but not essential.

- Nursing pads: These are an absolute must. (It is so embarrassing when you start leaking in public without them.) For the first couple of months I'd use the disposable ones. You can usually buy them in the baby section of your supermarket.

- Nursing bras: I didn't like the ones with underwires. I recommend the kind with a hook at the top, not a snap in the middle. (The snaps can come undone when you get engorged, and then your boob flies out. Not pretty.) A nursing gown can be nice, but I wasn't coordinated enough to use it for the first few weeks. I just pulled my shirt off so I could see what I was doing.

- Breast milk storage bags: Gerber Seal 'N Go are great.

- Breast pump: I recommend purchasing the Medela Pump In Style (advanced) or renting a hospital-grade one from a drugstore.

- Bottled water: I suggest keeping bottled water stashed all over the house, especially by your "nursing station." You will not believe how thirsty you can get while nursing, especially just when you've settled in and the baby is actually nursing and everything is going well . . . except that you are dying of thirst.

For the Car

- Window shade

- Rearview mirror to see the backseat

- Baby neck roll cushion: These are designed to support the baby's neck when he/she sleeps in the car seat or stroller.

- Car seat strap covers: The extra padding will make your baby more comfortable during car rides.

Miscellaneous Items

- Changing pad covers: The ones from Pottery Barn Kids are much softer than most, and Pee-Wee makes good disposable ones. Get at least three spare covers; you will need them in the first few weeks!

● Diaper bag: You will need two bags: one small bag for the quick errand and a big bag that will work for the entire day.

● Mattress pads: waterproof crib pads are great.

● Pacifier: If you're going to give your child pacifiers, try Nuk pacifiers for newborns (silicone, not latex). My kids didn't use pacifiers, but my friends swore these are the best.

● Sheet savers: Buy medium and large sizes for the changing table and crib.

● Sleep sack: These are better than blankets for newborns.

● Sleep support wedge: These can help babies sleep, but they are not necessary and you should ask your doctor about their thoughts on sleep positioners before purchasing one (some people worry about safety issues).

CLOTHES/LAYETTE

Baby hangers

Blankets (3 receiving, 2 for stroller)

Bunting (Lands' End has a cute one)/ snowsuit

Convertible nightgowns (these make it easy to change newborns at night)

Hats (1 fleece, 3 cotton)

Mittens/bundler (if you have a winter baby)

Onesies (10)

Pajamas (3); if you have a winter baby, get lots with long sleeves and footies (they outgrow the footies quickly).

Side-snapping shirts (6)

Socks (6–8, and just stick with all white at first)

Sweater (1)

TOILETRIES AND PHARMACY ITEMS FOR THE BATHROOM

Antibacterial ointment (I recommend bac-itracin.)

Baby grooming kit containing baby comb and brush, baby nail scissors and clipper, baby toothbrush

Baby wash

Batteries (A, AA, AAA, C, D, and 9-volt): You'll need these for the baby monitor and certain toys.

Cotton balls: for bris or cleaning belly button area

Diaper rash cream

Diapers: Purchase newborn-size diapers for your new baby. Get the ultrathin kind so you can easily tell when the diaper is wet. You probably won't need more than 100 of the newborn size since babies outgrow them fast, but if you buy too many you can always take them back to the store and trade them in for bigger sizes.

Gauze (various sizes)

Gauze squares: Wipes can be really hard on a baby's skin, so we used gauze and warm water to clean our baby for the first couple of weeks. Some experts say to use cotton balls, but then cotton can get all over the baby. Gauze squares are also useful for keeping ointment on a boy's circumcision scar. Get a wide-mouth thermos to keep water warm at the changing table, unless you enjoy running to the sink every time you change your child.

Hand sanitizer

Infant gas relief medicine (I recommend Mylicon.)

Infants' Tylenol

Laundry detergent: I recommend Dreft; it is a special gentle detergent that must be used for all clothing you are washing when the baby is small. Their skin is extremely sensitive. Also run the rinse cycle an extra time to ensure all traces of soap are removed.

Moisturizing lotion

Nasal aspirator

Ointment for dry, chafed skin (I like Aquaphor.)

Organic lotion and oil

Pedialyte

Rubbing alcohol

Saline drops (for baby's nose)

Small plastic bowl to wash baby

Stain remover

Thermometer

Trash can

Trash can liners

Wipes: I recommend purchasing sensitive wipes. Note: Don't bother buying a wipe warmer; it warms only the top wipe, and I find the baby doesn't notice the difference.

CHANGING STAND

Alcohol/alcohol prep pads (for belly button)

Burp cloths

Changing stand cover (plus an extra terry fitted changing table cover)

Chux pads: Use these on the changing stand and underneath the sheet on the crib so you don't need to change them all the time.

Cotton balls and gauze squares

Cotton swabs (for applying creams and cleaning special areas—not for ears!)

Diapers (keep a stack on the stand and your supply in the bathroom)

Diaper wipes

Hairbrush

Hats

Nightgowns

Ointment

Receiving blankets

Socks

Thermometer

Tissues

Trash can or Diaper Genie (with extra bags or Diaper Genie refill)

WHERE TO SHOP FOR BABY

Baby Gear

These retailers have everything and are great places to register.

- Babies "R" Us: babiesrus.com
- Baby Geared: babygeared.com
- BabyStyle: babystyle.com
- Buy Buy Baby: buybuybaby.com
- Giggle: egiggle.com

Clothing

Babies grow so quickly, you'll want to buy cute yet affordable clothes. After all, you'll be replacing them quickly. These are great places to shop for little ones.

- BabyGap: babygap.com
- Crew Cuts: jcrew.com/AST/Navigation/Crew Cuts.jsp
- Gymboree: gymboree.com
- Hanna Andersson: hannaandersson.com
- Lands' End: landsend.com
- Old Navy: oldnavy.com

Furniture

Here are some places to find cute, sturdy pieces for your child's room.

- Design Within Reach for Kids: dwr.com/category/accessories/kids.do
- Ikea: ikea.com
- The Land of Nod: landofnod.com
- Pottery Barn: potterybarnkids.com

Child Safety

You'll need to purchase various items to make your home safe for baby. These sites are great resources. They explain everything you need and tell you where to get it.

- Baby Proofer: mrbabyproofer.com/
- One Step Ahead: onestepahead.com/
- Perfectly Safe: perfectlysafe.com

Toys

Need I say more?

- ABC School Specialty: abcschoolsupply.com
- Baby Einstein: babyeinstein.com
- Barney's: barneys.com
- Cocoa Crayon: cocoacrayon.com
- Didi's Boutique: didis.net
- Disney: disneystore.com
- FAO Schwarz: fao.com
- Genius Jones: geniusjones.com
- Growing Tree Toys: growingtreetoys.com
- Kid O: kidOnyc.com
- Kidding Around: kiddingaround.us
- Modernseed: modernseed.com
- Scholastic Store: shop.scholastic.com
- Toys "R" Us: toysrus.com

HOSPITAL PACKING LIST

Now that your home is stocked and ready for baby, it's time to prep for the big delivery.

MOMMY

Nightgown

Bathrobe (a thin cotton one)

Underwear (five pairs)

Nursing bra

Sanitary pads

Slippers/flip-flops

Socks (three pairs)

Toiletry bag

Going home outfit

DADDY

Bathing suit (if he needs to get in the shower with you)

Pajamas

Slippers

Socks

Toiletry bag

BABY

Baby neck roll cushion

Blanket

Burp cloth

Diapers

Hat

Onesie

Pacifier

Side-snapping shirt

OTHER

Blanket

Cell phone charger

Cough drops (to soothe a throat that might be sore from yelling during labor)

Digital camera, battery charger

Flashlight or night-light: You will want to look at the baby at night, and the overhead light is so bright in the hospital you will be afraid to wake up the baby.

Flex straws (10)

Food (for after the delivery or a hungry daddy)

Hair bands

Honey (for sustenance during delivery)

iPod and charger

Letter for hospital regarding doula/labor assistant (if applicable)

Lip balm (your lips get dry during labor)

Money, including a roll of quarters (to buy food or newspapers, make phone calls, et cetera)

Pen and paper

Phone list of people to call when the baby arrives

Plastic trash bag (for transporting clothing, towels in and out of the hospital)

Presents for the nurses taking care of you: Going the extra mile will get you lots of things in the hospital.

Social Security number (yours and Daddy's)

Something to entertain you, like your favorite movies and DVD player or a stack of gossip magazines. Once the drugs have been administered, there's a lot of waiting.

Plastic utensils: If someone brings food post-delivery, you will be happy to have utensils to eat right away.

Stopwatch to time contractions

Towels: You will want to use your own towels when you take a shower.

Video camera, plus videotape for camera, if you want your labor and delivery filmed

Washcloths for cooling down

Water: You'll probably want to chug bottles, but your water intake may be restricted to ice.

ITEMS TO PACK AT THE LAST MINUTE

Cell phone

Medications (any medications that you and your husband take regularly)

Pillows with easily identifiable pillowcases. Yes, they have pillows at the hospital, but they are probably not as comfortable as yours and it will be a long time before you will get to sleep much again, so you might as well make the best of it.

Purse

Water

LABOR

During Labor To-Dos

1 Call your pediatrician and notify them you are in labor.

2 At the hospital, set up your shower products before you get your epidural or go into final stages of labor. You are not going to be interested in dragging out toiletries a few hours after delivering a baby.

3 Get excited!

Immediately After Labor To-Dos

1 Fill out the birth certificate. You will need your and the father of your child's Social Security numbers. The hospital will automatically apply for your child's Social Security number when you fill out the birth certificate. Note: If you do not fill it out at the hospital, you only have forty-eight hours to return it to the hospital or it will take several months to get a Social Security number for your child.

2 Get out your "poop, sleep, and eat journal." This is a notebook where you will start keeping track of your baby's bodily functions. Note: When your child poops within the first twenty-four hours, it will be black and mushy (this is meconium). Do not be alarmed. This is healthy.

3 Call your pediatrician after you have given birth so the doctor can come to the hospital. If your pediatrician is not available, the hospital pediatrician will see your child to do the necessary examinations for releasing your child from the hospital.

4 Tell the nurse if you do not want visitors when you are sleeping. Some people like to be woken up if someone comes to visit, some don't.

COMING HOME FROM THE HOSPITAL TO-DOS

The most important thing is to try to take it easy, especially the first few days. There will be people around who want to wait on you. Let them!

1 Put up a sign on your front door that says "Newborn in the house. Please wash hands and take off shoes."

2 Add the newest member of the family to your health insurance policy.

3 Write/rewrite your will and adjust your life insurance policy.

4 Keep a vigilant log of *everything* your child does the first few weeks: times of pees, poops, when you're feeding, how much baby ate, how long baby slept. That way, if there are any problems, you will be able to give the doctor specific information.

5 Keep a list of all gifts that arrive so when you get around to sending thank-you notes, you'll know who gave you what. More important, keep updating the list as gifts arrive, because people will be calling and asking you if you got the flowers, and you will want to be able to tell them, "Yes, the red roses were wonderful." You will be surprised how sensitive people are.

6 Try to put your photos into albums or onto CDs as soon as possible. Otherwise you might forget, and people really do want to see pictures of your new baby (including you, once you have time to look at the pictures!) when they come over to visit. I highly recommend shutter fly.com!

Additional Advice

1 When bottle feeding, do not under any circumstances rock the chair while you are feed-

ing the baby. Can you imagine trying to drink something while rocking?

2 When breast-feeding:

> Do not drink OJ; consume caffeine; eat tomatoes, onions, cabbage, chocolate, tuna fish, broccoli, or anything that gives you gas.

> If the child is tired and not sucking, tickle his cheek or back of his neck. Baby will regain interest in eating.

> If you have problems with milk coming in, drink thistle tea, milk, or beer (talk to your doctor or lactation specialist about drinking beer first, though, and never drink more than one. Also, dark beer is best).

> If your breasts become engorged, place cool cabbage leaves on them to reduce swelling.

3 Change your baby's diaper in the middle of the feeding. Otherwise she will fall asleep and wake up when you change her later.

4 Burp the baby *constantly* (pat with your fingers closed, not open, or you will create more gas).

5 Be careful not to hold anything—a phone, a book, anything—over the baby's head while feeding. It could slip and fall on the baby's head.

6 Keep your child in a nightgown with an open bottom for the first few weeks. It's *so* much easier to change the diapers (which you will be doing very frequently).

RESOURCES

BOOKS

The Baby Whisperer series, by Tracy Hogg and Melinda Blau

Dr. Spock's Baby and Child Care, 8th edition, by Benjamin Spock, M.D., and Robert Needleman, M.D.

The Girlfriends' Guide to Pregnancy, by Vicki Iovine

What to Expect When You're Expecting, 4th edition, by Heidi Murkoff and Sharon Mazel

The Womanly Art of Breastfeeding, 7th revised edition, by La Leche League International

MAGAZINES

American Baby

Cookie

Family Circle

Fit Pregnancy

Parenting

Parents

Pregnancy

Urban Baby & Toddler (Canadian magazine)

WEBSITES

Baby Center: babycenter.com

The Bump: thebump.com

Pregnancy Today: pregnancytoday.com

PARENTING

Soon after your return home from the hospital, you realize that your precious bundle of joy did not ship with an owner's manual or a customer support contact number. But that's okay because Mother Nature, in her infinite wisdom, has given us more innate resources than we could ever imagine. For those few things she may have forgotten, I am here to fill in the blanks.

Being a new mom, there was never anything more frustrating than packing up my little one for a stroll in the park. Inevitably, I would pack thirteen diapers but forget the wipes or to have refilled the Cheerios snack cup or myriad other incidental but overwhelmingly important items. My diaper bag was the evil hole where things went and never came back—until I got myself organized with a checklist of the essentials. I even laminated this list and threw it in the bag so that if Grandma or the babysitter needed to go out, there was a quick reference of all that should be there. The result? Happy baby, happier mommy!

DIAPER BAG CHECKLIST

- Antibiotic ointment
- Band-Aids
- Blanket
- Books
- Cell phone
- Change of clothing
- Children's Benadryl (for any possible allergic reactions)
- Diapers
- Emergency phone numbers card
- Hand sanitizer
- Health insurance card
- ID
- Money ($40)
- Paper
- Pen
- Snacks
- Tissues
- Toys
- Wipes

EXTRA ITEMS WHEN TRAVELING LONG-DISTANCE (IN THE CAR LONGER THAN THIRTY MINUTES!)

- Cell phone charger
- Coloring books
- Crayons
- DVD player, adapter, charger, movies

Headphones

Neck pillow

Pajamas

Sippy cup

Snacks (extra)

Thermometer

Video camera

CHORE CHART

Giving kids day-to-day chores teaches them to be responsible. Here's a chart I created to keep track of what needs to be done and when. Print one out for yourself or create one on a dry-erase board. Do whatever helps you teach your kids to pitch in!

DAY	CHORE	SIGNATURE
Monday	Make beds and help clean the house	
Tuesday	Help with laundry	
Wednesday	Clear dinner table	
Thursday	Clean room	
Friday	Set the table	

PARENTING

INSTRUCTIONS TO GIVE YOUR CHILD'S CAREGIVER (BABYSITTER, GRANDPARENT, ET AL.)

Let's face it: It can be nerve-racking to leave your kids in someone else's care. Here are a few tips to give your child caregiver that'll give *you* some peace of mind.

Safety Inside the Home

1 Do not write down the house alarm code anywhere.

2 Never turn off the alarm in front of anyone (you do not want even the plumber knowing the house alarm code).

3 Never open the door for strangers.

4 Never tell anyone who is calling that you are home alone with the children or that the parents are out of town.

5 Never leave the child alone in the bathtub for any reason—ever! There is nothing anyone could be calling about that is more important than the safety of the child. A child can drown in an inch of water.

6 If you are cooking, make sure you do not leave the stove on if you leave the kitchen. When you are done cooking, double-check that all appliances are turned off.

7 Always make sure the house is locked, garage door is shut, and alarm is on when you are home alone with the children.

Medications

1 Do not administer medication of any kind (even if it's over-the-counter) without first speaking to the parent.

2 Be sure to write down and keep a log of what medication was given and what dosage.

3 Always check the expiration date of the medication.

4 Put medication in a safe place out of reach of the children.

Safety Outside the Home

1 Do not speak to any strangers when you are with the children. It teaches them a bad habit and may put the children in a dangerous situation.

2 Never release the child to anyone, even a family member, without the consent of the parent.

Cars

1 Make sure the children always have their seat belts on.

2 Never leave the children alone in the car.

3 Never leave the keys to the car where the children can get hold of them.

Personal Requirements

1 Do not do personal errands with the children.

2 Keep personal phone calls to a minimum when you are with the children.

3 Never bring any friends/family members of yours into our home without permission.

Behavior in Front of Children

1 When you are with the children, always try to treat people respectfully. The children are watching you and learning from your behaviors.

2 Always encourage the children to tell the truth. We do not want them thinking it is okay to keep secrets or lie.

3 Do not allow children under two years old to watch TV.

4 Discipline children according to our family philosophy. (Be sure to discuss this thoroughly with the caregiver.)

Emergency Situations

No one wants to even think about their children having an emergency when they're not present. However, giving your caregiver the following instructions will improve the odds of a positive outcome.

1 In a life-threatening emergency, call 911 or the Poison Control Center before calling the

parents. A list of phone numbers are posted for emergency use by the kitchen phone.

2 Contact the parents immediately.

3 If the parents cannot be reached, contact the family's nearest relative or trusted friend. If the situation warrants immediate action or if the phones are inoperative, try to get assistance from the neighbors.

AUTHORIZATION TO TREAT A MINOR

Have your child caregiver sign and date two "Authorization to Treat a Minor" forms per child: One should be put on file at their pediatrician's office, the other held in the child care provider's possession. This form can be found online at everythingnanny.com/authorization_to_treat.htm.

In the unlikely event of an emergency, if the parents cannot be reached by the child care provider, the doctor, and/or the hospital, this allows the doctor to ask permission of the child care provider to administer any necessary medical care to the children. It also establishes that the child care provider is required to give authorization to medical personnel to treat the children, and the parents understand that all medical care administered would be on the advice and at the discretion of *medical personnel only.*

PARENTING

FAMILY INFORMATION TO SHARE WITH YOUR CHILD'S CAREGIVER

1 Daily routine (bedtime routines, meals, et cetera)

2 Weekly after-school activities (for example, sports programs)

3 Homework and school requirements

4 Special interests of the children

5 Food requirements

6 Medical issues (illnesses, allergies, regular medication)

7 Religious requirements (for example, special dietary restrictions for certain holidays)

8 List of emergency contact numbers

9 List of family doctors

10 The children's favorite books, TV shows, computer and video games

11 List of the children's friends

12 Upcoming important events (birthday parties, family vacations, et cetera)

BABYSITTERS

Interview Questionnaire

1 Tell me a little about yourself. Where did you grow up? Did you have brothers and sisters?

2 When you aren't working, what do you like to do? Do you have any hobbies?

3 How old were the kids in your last job?

4 What types of activities did you do with them?

5 What were the kids' favorite foods? Favorite books?

6 What was a typical day? What were your hours?

7 How long did you work there? (Get exact dates.)

8 What were your responsibilities?

9 What was the most difficult situation you were in with the children?

10 Were you ever in an emergency situation with the children? If yes, how did you handle the situation?

11 Did you travel with the family? If yes, where? What were your responsibilities?

12 Did the parents ever go out of town and leave you with the children?

13 Why do you want to leave?

14 Are you still employed?

15 If yes, do they know you are not happy? Have you tried to talk to them? If so, what did they say? Do they know you are looking for a job? What are they going to say when you tell them you have another job?

16 If no, when did you leave? Why did you leave?

17 Could I call your former employer? If yes, what do you think they will tell me about you?

18 Do you smoke? If yes, how often?

19 Do you drive? If yes, when was the last time? Are you comfortable driving on the highway? Do you have your own car? Have you ever been in any accidents?

20 Can you swim? When was the last time you swam? In a pool? In an ocean?

21 Do you have any medical conditions or any allergies that would affect your ability to do your job?

22 Can you cook? If yes, how often did you cook? What did you cook?

23 Do you know CPR?

24 Do you have any responsibilities or commitments that would prevent you from staying late or working weekends?

Questions for References

1 How long was she with you?

2 Why did she leave?

3 What was she like with the children?

4 Would you hire her again?

5 Was she sick often? Did she take a lot of personal time off?

6 If you had to name three negative qualities about her, what would they be?

7 What were her responsibilities? Did she do more than take care of children (clean, cook, drive, run errands, et cetera)?

8 Was there ever an emergency or difficult situation that she had to handle on her own?

9 Did she give you daily feedback on your children? Did she take instruction well?

10 Do you work? What do you do? Were either you or your husband home during the day, or was she pretty much on her own?

11 Were you around when she was with the children?

12 Did you ever go out of town and leave them with her?

13 How much were you paying her?

14 How would you describe her response to requests (takes her time, moves slowly, fast, et cetera)?

PRESCHOOL INTERVIEW GUIDE

Nursery School Assessment Questions for Parents

The following three lists have been compiled, with slight modifications, from Victoria Goldman's website, articles, and book, *The Manhattan Directory of Private Nursery Schools* (6th edition), published by Soho Press, Inc. © copyright 2007, excerpted by permission of Victoria Goldman and Soho Press, Inc. Please note that many of the answers to the questions below might be found in brochures and on websites, but feel free to ask a school representative any of the questions listed below.

1 Are the teachers working on the floor with the children or do they keep their distance?

2 What are the toilet facilities like, and are they separate for adults?

3 Are the indoor and outdoor areas spacious enough for children to move and play with ease?

4 Are the teachers warm?

5 Does the school allow parents in the classroom?

6 At what age does the school introduce phonics, the alphabet, numbers, formal lessons?

7 Do the teachers use learning games?

8 Are the children required to join activities?

9 Does the school provide lunch?

10 What kinds of snacks are served?

11 If meals and/or snacks are served, are they nutritious?

12 Are naps mandatory or can the children just rest quietly?

13 How are sick children cared for?

14 Are there opportunities for parent involvement?

15 Are there workshops for parents?

16 How often during the year are parent-teacher conferences scheduled?

17 How long do parent-teacher conferences last? (They can vary from fifteen minutes to two and a half hours.)

18 What is the child-teacher ratio?

19 How many children are in a typical class?

20 What kind of professional qualifications do teachers and administrators have?

21 What is teacher turnover like?

PARENTING

22 What kind of security measures are employed around the school building and grounds?

23 How are drop-off and dismissal handled? (I recommend observing these systems firsthand.)

24 Does the school accommodate early drop-off or late pickup?

25 Is play equipment safe and well-maintained?

26 Are there field trips and neighborhood outings? How are parents notified? Who chaperones the children? How are they transported and supervised?

27 Do the children use public playgrounds and parks? If so, how are they supervised and transported to and from?

28 How many times during the year do parents have formal teacher conferences and written reports?

29 How does the school handle the separation process and what kind of transition schedule is used to allow children to become familiar with the classroom, teachers, and other students (visits, phasing into a full schedule)?

30 What kind of extras are offered: music, art, swimming, dance, cooking, et cetera?

31 What types of physical activities do children participate in? Are they required to participate?

32 Is community service part of the curriculum?

33 What kind of extracurricular and after-school activities are offered by or at the school?

34 How is religious training integrated into daily activities?

35 Do you offer school tours?

36 How will the time be organized during my scheduled school visit with my child?

37 Are children exposed to or introduced to other languages? At what age?

38 Is there a summer program?

39 Will our family values, beliefs, and customs be supported?

40 What makes this school unique from all the rest?

41 Is there standardized testing? Starting at what age?

42 How are individual birthdays celebrated?

43 Is it more of a play school or work school?

44 Are there both structured and open-ended activities?

45 Are children encouraged to ask questions and become active problem solvers?

46 Does the school provide daily written or oral communication about a child's eating, sleeping, and developmental achievements?

47 Does each child work at his or her own pace?

48 Is there a structured circle time?

Note: It's a good idea to let the administrator know if their school is your first choice and to send a follow-up letter stating that.

Typical Questions Asked During the Parent Interview

1 What do you do together as a family?

2 What are your child's weekly activities?

3 What are your child's favorite activities?

4 What are your child's strengths?

5 What are your child's weaknesses?

6 What is important to you in your child's education?

7 What books does your child like?

8 What is your understanding of education? (Correct answer: teach the right values.)

9 How would you describe your child?

Advice from a School Counselor

Here are some tips from a school counselor that will help you ace your interviews.

1 Know your child really well.

2 Discuss exactly what your child likes and dislikes, in terms of:

> What your child loves to do
>
> What excites your child
>
> What is most fun for your child
>
> Who spends time with your child
>
> Who reads to your child
>
> Is your child better in the morning or afternoon

3 Discuss what you want in an education.

> The right answer is: "I want what is developmentally correct for my child. That means, if you can push her, then push her, but we're happy with whatever her developmental progress is."
>
> Also, tell the interviewer you have heard that the school is very academic but gives the children a lot of care.

4 Be very interested in the school. Ask questions.

5 Remember, the interviewer will be sizing you up every time they meet with you. They will ask you the same questions in different ways; be consistent.

6 The dress code for the interview is business casual. Many parents show up in suits, which is fine. Just do *not* wear jeans.

7 Know everything possible about your child and be clear that you are very involved with his or her life and spend a lot of time with him or her.

> *Do not* say "We're in the office all the time, but we have great child care." The schools want to hear that you, the parents, are the primary caregivers.

8 Emphasize that you are happy to participate in school activities. For example, you would make the time to participate in school functions, you would be happy to come in to your child's class and do a presentation on what it's like to be a fashion designer.

9 Explain that you want to be involved with the school directly and that you want to hear developmental feedback from the teachers directly.

10 Schools want to know that if something goes wrong, they can reach the parents directly and that you will make yourselves immediately available.

11 The school wants to hear that you read to your child. This is important.

Again, remember: *They will be sizing you up every time they meet with you. They are judging if you are good, involved parents.*

RESOURCES

Since I've included an extensive list of books on the subject of parenting, I'll list the magazines and websites first. You can consult these while you have your new bookshelf installed!

MAGAZINES

Child (very similar to *Parenting*): child.com

Cookie (hip/cool parenting magazine): cookiemag.com

Parenting (great monthly magazine that covers issues for children of all ages): parenting.com

WEBSITES

HEALTH CARE

American Academy of Pediatrics: aap.org

iVillage: parenting.ivillage.com

KidsHealth: kidshealth.org

SAFETY

123 Safe: 123safe.com

Kids in Danger: kidsindanger.org

TRAVEL

BabyCenter: babycenter.com

Centers for Disease Control: cdc.gov/travel

Expedia: expedia.com/daily/family

Family on Board: familyonboard.com

Family Travel Forum: familytravelforum.com

International Association for Medical Assistance to Travellers: iamat.org

Merck: merck.com/mmhe/print/sec25/ch303/ch303a.html

My Lifeguard for Health: mylifeguardforhealth.com

Safe Kids: safekids.org

GENERAL

Daily Candy Kids: dailycandy.com/kids/everywhere

Goop: goop.com (Gwyneth Paltrow offers tips for kid friendly activities)

Momcierge: momcierge.com

BOOKS

I'm not going to dole out parenting advice, but you may find the following books to be helpful or of interest. Please note that these lists are from parenting expert Jean Kunhardt's Soho Parenting website and have been reprinted with permission and adapted to be more accessible.

PARENTING

Best Friends, Worst Enemies: Understanding the Social Lives of Children, by Michael Thompson and Catherine O'Neill Grace with Lawrence J. Cohen

The Blessing of a Skinned Knee: Using Jewish Teachings to Raise Self-Reliant Children, by Wendy Mogel

The Emotional Life of the Toddler, by Alicia F. Lieberman

Healthy Sleep Habits, Happy Child, by Marc Weissbluth

The Hurried Child: 25th Anniversary Edition, by David Elkind

Nurturing Good Children Now: 10 Basic Skills to Protect and Strengthen Your Child's Core Self, by Ron Taffel with Melinda Blau

1–2–3 Magic: Effective Discipline for Children 2–12, by Thomas W. Phelan

Parenting by Heart: How to Stay Connected to Your Child in a Disconnected World, by Ron Taffel with Melinda Blau

Parenting, Inc.: How the Billion-Dollar Baby Business Has Changed the Way We Raise Our Children, by Pamela Paul

The Power of Play: Learning What Comes Naturally, by David Elkind

MARRIAGE AFTER BECOMING PARENTS

PARENTING

The Art of Marriage Maintenance, by Sylvia R. Karasu and T. Byram Karasu

Baby-proofing Your Marriage: How to Laugh More, Argue Less and Communicate Better as Your Family Grows, by Stacie Cockrell, Cathy O'Neill, and Julia Stone.

Getting the Love You Want: A Guide for Couples, 20th Anniversary Edition, by Harville Hendrix

How Can I Get Through to You?: Closing the Intimacy Gap Between Men and Women, by Terrence Real

Hump: True Tales of Sex After Kids, by Kimberly Ford

The Intimacy Factor: The Ground Rules for Overcoming the Obstacles to Truth, Respect, and Lasting Love, by Pia Mellody and Lawrence S. Freundlich

The New Rules of Marriage: What You Need to Know to Make Love Work, by Terrence Real

Passionate Marriage: Keeping Love and Intimacy Alive in Committed Relationships, by David Schnarch

Ten Lessons to Transform Your Marriage: America's Love Lab Experts Share Their Strategies for Strengthening Your Relationship, by John M. Gottman, Julie Schwartz Gottman, and Joan DeClaire.

PARENTING

The Bitch in the House: 26 Women Tell the Truth About Sex, Solitude, Work, Motherhood, and Marriage, edited by Cathi Hanauer

Buddha Mom: The Path of Mindful Mothering, by Jacqueline Kramer

Don't Just Stand There: How to Be Helpful, Clued-In, Supportive, Engaged, Meaningful, and Relevant in the Delivery Room, by Elissa Stein and Jon Lichtenstein

Flux: Women on Sex, Work, Love, Kids, and Life in a Half-Changed World, by Peggy Orenstein

I Don't Know How She Does It, by Allison Pearson

It's a Boy: Women Writers on Raising Sons, edited by Andrea J. Buchanan

It's a Girl: Women Writers on Raising Daughters, by Andrea J. Buchanan

The Mask of Motherhood: How Becoming a Mother Changes Our Lives and Why We Never Talk About It, by Susan Maushart

Maternal Desire: On Children, Love, and the Inner Life, by Daphne de Marneffe

Misconceptions: Truth, Lies, and the Unexpected on the Journey to Motherhood, by Naomi Wolf

The Mommy Myth: The Idealization of Motherhood and How It Has Undermined All Women, by Susan Douglas and Meredith W. Michaels

Mother Reader: Essential Writings on Motherhood, edited by Moyra Davey

A Mother's Circle: An Intimate Dialogue on Becoming a Mother, by Sandra Kunhardt Basile with Jean Kunhardt and Lisa Spiegel.

Mother Shock: Loving Every (Other) Minute of It, edited by Andrea J. Buchanan

Mothers Who Think: Tales of Real-Life Parenthood, edited by Camille Peri and Kate Moses

The Price of Motherhood: Why the Most Important Job in the World Is Still the Least Valued, by Ann Crittenden

The Truth Behind the Mommy Wars: Who Decides What Makes a Good Mother? by Miriam Peskowitz

PUBERTY, SEXUALITY, AND KIDS' CHANGING BODIES

Asking About Sex and Growing Up: A Question-and-Answer Book for Boys and Girls, by Joanna Cole

The Care & Keeping of You: The Body Book for Girls (American Girl Library), by Valorie Schaefer and Norm Bendell

Dr. Ruth Talks to Kids: Where You Came From, How Your Body Changes, and What Sex Is All About, by Dr. Ruth Westheimer

Girl in the Mirror: Mothers and Daughters in the Years of Adolescence, by Nancy L. Snyderman and Peg Streep

PARENTING

How to Talk to Your Child About Sex: It's Best to Start Early, But It's Never Too Late—A Step-by-Step Guide for Every Age, by Linda Eyre and Richard Eyre

It's Perfectly Normal: Changing Bodies, Growing Up, Sex, and Sexual Health (Robie Sex Books), by Robie H. Harris

It's So Amazing!: A Book About Eggs, Sperm, Birth, Babies, and Families (Robie Sex Books), by Robie H. Harris

My Body, My Self for Girls: A "What's Happening to My Body?" Book, Second Edition, by Lynda Madaras and Area Madaras

Raising Cain: Protecting the Emotional Life of Boys, by Dan Kindlon and Michael Thompson

Ready, Set, Grow!: A "What's Happening to My Body?" Book for Younger Girls, by Lynda Madaras

What's Going On Down There?: Answers to Questions Boys Find Hard to Ask, by Karen Gravelle with Nick and Chava Castro

The "What's Happening to My Body?" Book for Boys, by Lynda Madaras with Area Madaras

"Where Did I Come From?", by Peter Mayle

PARENTING SIBLINGS: BOOKS FOR PARENTS AND KIDS

From One Child to Two: What to Expect, How to Cope, and How to Enjoy Your Growing Family, by Judy Dunn

I'm a Big Brother, by Joanna Cole

I'm a Big Sister, by Joanna Cole

Julius, the Baby of the World, by Kevin Henkes

Loving Each One Best: A Caring and Practical Approach to Raising Siblings, by Nancy Samalin with Catherine Whitney

The New Baby, by Mercer Mayer

The New Baby at Your House, by Joanna Cole

Siblings Without Rivalry: How to Help Your Children Live Together So You Can Live Too, by Adele Faber and Elaine Mazlish

Will There Be a Lap for Me?, by Dorothy Corey

You're the Boss, Baby Duck!, by Amy Hest

TRAVEL

I love to travel. I love to see new places, eat new foods, and, of course, shop. However, my love of travel is almost equal in measure to my aversion to packing. I have often thought that my ideal vacation spot would be a nudist resort. Sunscreen? Packed! And not much else.

But alas, travel planning and packing are the prices one pays to delight the senses with new experiences. That being said, nothing can kill a good time like forgetting your antinausea medication or realizing, in midair, that you never reconfirmed your hotel reservation.

Follow my handy guide to preparing for your trip and, whether you are a senior or taking along Junior, you will be on the road to fun and adventure! And if you're still not into packing after reading this chapter, follow the advice of my first boss who always told me that I could forget anything as long as I have my credit card, passport, and driver's license. You can always buy the rest!

International Travel To-Dos

- Give someone a photocopy of your passport in case you lose yours.

- Let your friends and family know if you are traveling somewhere that falls in a different time zone and make sure they know exactly what the time difference is. For example, make it clear that you are six hours ahead of their time so they don't wake you up in the middle of the night with a phone call.

- Check to see if you need a visa to enter your destination country. This and other important travel information can easily be found at www .travel.state.gov/.

- Consider converting some of your dollars to foreign money before you leave on your trip. The exchange rate is sometimes better in the United States.

- Check to see if you need to get any vaccinations before you visit your destination country.

- You might need to take copies of your prescriptions as some countries will ask for proof that you need the medications and that they are yours.

- Make sure your cell phone is set up for international dialing (and texting if you're a texter—this is a separate request). Check international rates with your phone carrier.

TRAVEL

Airline To-Dos

- Check weight restrictions for luggage. Most international airlines have weight restrictions but will take your overweight luggage if you are willing to pay a penalty fee.

- Check tickets carefully the day of departure in case there's been a change in carriers.

- Very often airlines code share flights. This means that one airline operates the flight and a partner airline sold you the flight. Request the name of the dominant airline so you know the correct terminal to go to for check-in, and ask your carrier which airline is operating the flight. Be sure to know your frequent flyer number for corresponding airline partner carriers, especially when flying overseas. You will want to earn miles for your trip.

- If you are planning on carrying on your luggage, think about how heavy your bag is. It could be a long walk to your connection!

- As soon as you arrive at the airport, check the departure boards for your departing terminal and correct gate. Gates are subject to change, so don't assume the gate printed on your ticket is correct.

Accommodations To-Dos

• Be sure to ask if there are any extra service charges or taxes on top of the accommodation fee before you book it. This could add up to 20 percent to the room fee. Get a confirmation of your reservation from the hotel directly (not from the travel agent).

• If you are traveling abroad, make sure the hotel quotes you in dollars how much the fee is. Also, find out the difference in price between a regular room and a suite. Sometimes it's just $20 to $30; and there can be a huge difference in the size of the room and/or the quality of your view.

• If you know you will arrive late at your hotel, be sure to contact the hotel front desk and ask that they make a note of your late arrival plans. This way you won't lose your accommodations.

• Get all your special requests (nonsmoking, extra cot, no aerosol spraying, et cetera) in writing from the hotel and be sure to bring this confirmation page with you, in case there is a problem.

• Request early check-in or late check-out if needed.

• Research the locations and phone numbers of the hospital and pharmacy closest to your hotel.

Rental Car To-Dos

• Ask if your rental company offers express check-in. Car rental lines can be miserably long.

- Make sure you understand all of the insurance options before you sign the paperwork. The rental company's insurance can be a big rip-off and your own car insurance might be sufficient. Or you might want to get additional insurance to "walk away" from any possible damage. That way you will not involve your own insurance company.

- Find out the return procedure in advance so you're not rushing at the last minute.

- Make sure all your paperwork is filled out ahead of time; fax a copy of your driver's license to the rental company if possible. Anything and everything you can do ahead of time will be beneficial. Be ready to present your rental car membership card, driver's license, and credit card when you pick up your car.

- If there is a phone in the car, be sure to find out what the number is.

- If there isn't a phone in the car, bring your own phone charger, iPod, and the necessary hookup cables. Find out if having a navigation system in your car is an option.

- Confirm that the car has air-conditioning. Believe it or not, the answer could be no.

- Foreign countries have vehicles with manual versus automatic transmissions. Be sure to state which kind you want.

TIMELINE

Seven to Ten Days Prior to Leaving for a Trip

- Get cash or traveler's checks if necessary.

- Take care of any beauty appointments.

- Cancel any recurring appointments you will miss.

- Type up an itinerary and a list of important phone numbers needed for the trip. Include emergency phone numbers and the number of the nearest consulate if you are traveling abroad.

- Start thinking about what you want to pack and tie up any loose ends (i.e., pick up items you want to take from the dry cleaner).

- Alert friends and/or family that you will be out of town.

Two Days Before Departure

- If traveling abroad, alert credit card companies that you are traveling overseas. For all trips, let them know that you will be charging more than usual so they don't suspend your card due to suspicious activity.

- Put a hold on any delivery services (mail and newspapers) if you're going to be away for more than a few days.

- Set a timer for the lights in your house so they come on at night and it appears you are home.

- Alert your neighbors that you will be out of town; ask them to be watchful.

- Prepay your bills that might come due in your absence.

- Check the weather report for your destination so you will pack appropriately.

- Refill any medication you will need for travel.

- Pack! (See packing checklist on page 156.)

One Day Before Departure

- Reconfirm all hotel reservation requests.

- Reconfirm your seat assignments with the airline and ask to be added to the standby upgrade lists.

- Set your email on auto-reply.

- Be sure you know how to check your email and voice mail messages from anywhere in the world.

- Give a spare house key to a family member, friend, or neighbor in case of emergency.

- Water your plants.

- Empty your garbage cans.

- Empty the washer and dryer.

- Hide your jewelry, valuables, and important financial documents.

- Charge your cell phone, BlackBerry, and any other electronic devices you want to take.

TRAVEL

- Print out directions to your destination and any phone numbers you may need.

- Give your contact information to family or close friends so they can get in touch with you in case of emergency.

- Clean out the refrigerator.

- Run the dishwasher.

Day of Departure

- Turn off air-conditioning or turn down heat.

- Unplug all major appliances.

- Turn off the washing machine water valve to avoid flooding.

- Check the oven and stove to make sure they're completely off.

- Check all doors and windows to make sure they are closed, locked, and secure.

- Throw out garbage.

- Be sure to pack all of your medication in your carry-on bag in case your luggage gets lost.

- Pack snacks to bring on the plane with you in case there are delays, and *especially* if you have young children.

- Check in for your flight online. This will save you time standing in line at the airport.

- Confirm that your flight is on time and what terminal/gate you are departing from.

- Make sure younger kids are wearing Velcro-closure or slip-on shoes. This makes it much easier to go through airport security.

- Tidy up (it's always nice to come home to a clean house).

- Set the alarm.

- Lock the house.

- Have fun!

After the Trip

- Reinstate all your deliveries.

- Plug in appliances.

- Try to spend the day after your trip as a vacation day or come home on the weekend so you can take care of everything that needs to be taken care of.

- Schedule a massage (traveling is stressful).

- Make a photo album of your trip.

PHONE NUMBERS TO TRAVEL WITH

If possible, bring email addresses as well, when applicable.

> Airline (the 800 number); also know your frequent flier number.

> Car rental company

> Cell phone numbers of everyone traveling with you; know their passport numbers as well.

TRAVEL

Concierge

Credit card companies, in the event your cards are lost or stolen

Doctors (all family doctors)

Family and friends at destination

Family to call in case of emergency

Friends to call in case of emergency

Hotel phone and fax number

Nearest consulate in case your passport is lost or stolen

Nearest hospital. Have the address, too.

Nearest pharmacy. Have the address and fax number.

Restaurants where you have reservations

Travel agent

PACKING

CARRY-ON

Any medication you might need during the flight

Change of clothing

Jewelry

Reading materials (books, magazines)

Reading glasses

Snacks

Socks

Wide scarf or sweater

Electronics

- BlackBerry or PDA charger
- Cell phone charger
- Computer and power plug
- Digital camera charger
- Extra memory card (1)
- Headphones (2 pairs)
- Headphone splitter
- iPod
- Kindle
- Portable DVD player (if you aren't bringing a computer)
- Video camera

ITEMS TO GO IN A SMALL PURSE INSIDE YOUR CARRY-ON

- BlackBerry or PDA
- Business cards
- Camera
- Cash, traveler's checks
- Cell phone
- Copy of contacts list (see page 155 for what goes on this list)
- Copy of itinerary
- Hand sanitizer
- Jewelry

Passports

Pens and paper

Plane tickets

Sunglasses

Wallet/money

Note: Remember that you can carry only four small bottles of liquid (no more than 3 ounces each) in your carry-on luggage, and they must be in a gallon-size clear plastic bag when you go through security.

Checked Baggage

Tip: Tag your suitcase with a brightly colored label, ribbon, scarf, buckled strap, or decal, so it is easy to differentiate from all the other luggage at baggage claim.

CLOTHING

Travel outfit for departure

Travel outfit for return

Any special clothing needed for specific activities on trip (e.g., wedding, party, boating)

Underwear

Bras

T-shirts

Socks

Evening outfits

Evening shoes

Jeans

Long sleeve T-shirts

Sweaters

Tennis shoes

Pajamas

Everyday shoes you can walk around in

Workout clothing

Note: Consider whether you need to pack special undergarments, hosiery, and/or a bathrobe, and add items accordingly.

MISCELLANEOUS ITEMS

Large duffel bag (in case you come back with more items than you left with—hey, I told you I like to shop!)

Raincoat, rain hat, umbrella

Movies (DVDs)

Laundry bag

Hair dryer

Travel guides and kid-friendly books about the trip (if applicable)

Gifts (if applicable)

TRAVEL

ELECTRONICS

Camera

iPod car adapter

iPod car charger

iPod travel speakers

Extra memory cards (2)

Extra videos for video camera (2)

Video camera cable to TV

Video camera charger

If traveling overseas, add

European adapters

European power strips for multiple charging devices

WARM WEATHER

Flip-flops or sandals

Bathing suits

Bathing suit cover-ups

Sun hat

Beach bag with the following contents:

Business cards

Pen

Sunscreen

Sun protection for the lips

Notepad

Mirror

Comb/brush

Hair bands

Insect repellent

COLD WEATHER

Winter coat

Hat

Scarf

Gloves

Boots

TOILETRY BAG (PUT THE FOLLOWING IN SEPARATE PLASTIC ZIPLOCK BAGS)

Bag 1: Shower

Shampoo

Conditioner

Soap

Comb

Shower cap

Razor

Shaving cream/gel

TRAVEL

Bag 2: After Shower

Deodorant

Hairbrush

Hair bands

Face lotion

Body lotion

Q-tips

Dental floss

Toothbrush

Toothpaste

Mouthwash

Aftershave or cologne

Bag 3: Miscellaneous

Woolite

Night-light/flashlight (with new battery)

Earplugs

Eyeglasses cleaning cloth

Tampons and pads

Mints

Bag 4: Makeup

Lipstick

Blush and blush brush

Makeup remover

Mascara

Eye shadow and/or liner

Tweezers

Magnifying mirror

Bag 5: Beauty Needs

Cuticle clipper

Nail clipper

Clear nail polish

Color nail polish

Nail file

Nail polish remover

Hair products

Blow-dryer (sometimes the dryers in the hotels are not strong enough)

PHARMACY ITEMS

When packing a portable medicine chest, be sure to include your preferred medications to treat the following:

Allergies

Cold/flu

Constipation

Cough

Diahrrea

Indigestion

Infections

Minor cuts

Nausea

Pain and fever

Rashes

Sleep
Note: Always check with your doctor prior to taking any drugs.

Kids' Packing List

NEWBORN TO EIGHTEEN MONTHS

Nipples (10)

Bottles (10)

Sterilizer

Changing pads

Burp cloths

Rice cereal (box)

Stroller

Diapers (2 packs per week)

Box of wet wipes (1 box per week)

Baby monitor

Portable crib and sheets

Car seat

Diaper bag (packed with all the usual items plus extra money)

Pacifiers

iPod with portable speakers

Bottle brush

Formula

Bathtub toys

Teething items (rattles, et cetera)

Laundry bag

Paper towels (for bottle drying, et cetera)

Plastic bags for dirty diapers

EIGHTEEN MONTHS TO THREE YEARS

Potty or potty seat

Diapers and wipes (if needed)

Swim diapers if applicable (2 per day)

Swim vest or floaties (if applicable)

Stroller

Bed railing

Baby monitor

Plastic dishes, spoons, sippy cups

Car seat

MISCELLANEOUS FOR KIDS OF ALL AGES

Sunblock

Snacks

Bug spray

List of emergency numbers

Copy of health insurance card

Dr. Spock's Baby and Child Care

Ziplock plastic bags

Passport

Favorite item to sleep with

Portable DVD player and headphones

DVDs

Backpack for kids three years and up (they like to feel as if they have their own luggage with them, too)

Sunglasses

TOYS TO CONSIDER

Beach toys

Crayons

Washable markers

Paper

Coloring books

Stickers

Miniature cars and dolls

Action figures

Dolls

Deck of cards

Maps

iPod with kids' games and movies

Video games

TOILETRIES

Cold medicine

Nail clippers

Band-Aids

Antibiotic ointment

Hand sanitizer

Comb

Baby oil

Kid shampoo

Woolite

Anti-itch cream

Fever medication

Thermometer

Toothbrush

Toothpaste

Hairbrush

Medicine for upset stomach

Cotton swabs

KIDS' CLOTHING FOR ONE WEEK (ALL TRIPS)

Underwear (12)

Socks (12)

Sweatpants (3)

Sweatshirts (3)

Jeans (3)

Long sleeve T-shirts (7)

Pajamas (7)

Hats (2)

Sweaters (3)

Belts (2)

Short-sleeve T-shirts (8)

Bathing suits (if applicable) (6)

Shirts (4)

Summer shirts (if applicable) (5)

Pants (cotton, et cetera) (5)

Shorts (8)

Nice outfits

Sandals (if applicable)

Flip-flops (if applicable)

Pairs of tennis shoes (3)

Raincoat

RESOURCES

BOOKS

1,000 Places to See Before You Die, by Patricia Schultz

Fodor's guides

Frommer's travel guides

Hip Hotels series, by Herbert Ypina

Zagat guides

WEBSITES

PICKING YOUR DESTINATION

Worldatlas.com

iescape.com

BOOKING YOUR FLIGHT

Bing.com/travel

Avoiddelays.com

Seatguru.com

Expedia.com

Travelocity.com

Orbitz.com

Kayak.com

BOOKING HOTELS

hiphotels.com

Tablethotels.com

Kayak.com

Bookingbuddies.com

RESEARCH

Fabsearch.com

Family-travel.co.uk

Fodors.com

Frommers.com

Concierge.com

Travelandleisure.com

Info.com

TRAVEL

CHILD CARE AND TRAVEL EASY

Care.com

Babiestravellite.com

Baby-equipment-rental.com

Deliciousbaby.com

Travelforkids.com

Travelmuse.com

MEDICAL ISSUES

Wellnessconcierge.com

TECHNOLOGY

Deadcellzones.com

OTHER HELPFUL SITES

50thingsandbeyond.com

Weather.com

TRAVEL

CARS

Isn't there a tiny part of you that still longs for a time when you could take your dad to the car dealership, kick a few tires, and come home with a new set of wheels? I used to think the big dealerships and commercials with all the fine print were intimidating, until I went through the very empowering process of researching and helping a friend buy a car.

The obvious first steps are to assess your needs and your budget. Whether you are buying a new or used car or have decided to lease, keep in mind that there are tricks to getting the best deals. Once you get your car, you will need to insure it. While this too may seem like a headache, my checklists will make it a breeze. Finally, since good maintenance is the best insurance for your car's life, I have included a punch list of items that will need to be serviced at 3,000, 10,000, 20,000, 30,000, and 50,000 miles. Readers, start your engines.

Purchasing and Selling a Car Initial To-Dos

• A dealer gives the best deals at the end of the month. They need to make their monthly numbers and there are new cars arriving, so they will want to get rid of their current inventory. So try to plan your new car search accordingly.

• Consider buying a car that has a few hundred (or a few thousand) miles on it. This will save you a significant amount of money since it will be "gently" used but (hopefully) still in near-mint condition.

• Do your homework. Check out websites for information (see page 183 for a list of sites)

• Familiarize yourself with the following terms. You should know these before you walk into a dealership:

- MSRP: manufacturer's suggested retail price (i.e., the full retail asking price)

- Tissue: what the car cost the dealer

- Rebate: money the manufacturer will give you toward a lease or sale

- Loyalty: discount, rebates, or other favorable terms the manufacturer will give you toward your next purchase or lease

Once you've figured out which car you want, go to a dealer (preferably one you probably won't buy from) and:

1 Test drive the car and take notes.

2 Get the paint code of the color you want. Note: You will pay a little more for metallic.

3 Ask if the car is a special edition. For example, sport or luxury cars have a different pricing structure.

4 Ask about the "package" and what is included. Some dealers will make you pay extra for something that is already included in the package; for example, navigation.

Closing the Deal

Now that you have all of the info, march into the dealer's office and negotiate. Here are two tips to remember:

• Always ask if there is a demo car available to sell (you will get a discount on it). If you choose a demo, make sure you get an extended warranty.

• When you have the deal you want and you're in their office closing, ask for the tire and rim guarantee. They'll probably throw it in for free.

Leasing

In addition to the above:

• Go on the manufacturer's website and see what price it is offering.

• Always ask for the pull-ahead program. This means the dealer will call you to come in three to six months before your lease is over and get you in a new car without paying your last payments. Therefore, you will get a newer car earlier.

- Key things to know when considering a lease:

Programs are determined by a certain number of miles you plan to put on your car per year. With lower miles come the best deals and lower prices. Do not over-estimate the number of miles you will need. You will pay for something you do not use. If you go slightly over, it is cheaper to pay the penalty than to buy more miles than you'll use.

The term to hold a car is 24, 36, 39, or 48 months.

Ask the dealer to put the buy-back price in your lease. You want to make sure this goes in because if you decide to purchase your car at the end of the lease, it gives you the value.

You are responsible for all repairs and up-keep of your car. The dealer will charge you if there are any major problems with the car, but the unofficial rule is this: If the visible damage spans less than four inches, they'll usually let it slide. So if there is bumper rash and tiny nicks, they will not penalize you. However, if there's a big crack in the windshield, you will have to pay.

Ask for a protection plan in the lease. This will ensure that service and maintenance are covered for the life of the lease.

Beware of hidden fees at the end and at the beginning of the lease. You can usually negotiate your way out of these, especially if you are a repeat customer.

If You Plan to Buy a Used Car

1 Go to www.cars.com, www.autotrader.com, and www.ebay.com to learn the car's current value.

2 Always have an independent mechanic or a local dealer (not the one you're buying from) check out the car for any problems before you buy.

3 If you buy from a dealer, ask for an extended warranty.

4 Ask the dealer for all service records.

5 Go to www.carfax.com to see if the car has ever been in an accident. Note: You will need the VIN—vehicle identification number—to get the info on this site.

6 Look up the "Blue Book" value on www .kbb.com.

Note: You might pay an additional tax on a car when you buy it privately (check your state laws).

Selling a Car To-Dos

1 Remember that selling a car yourself will always bring a better price than if you sold it back to a dealer.

2 Look at the price of other cars similar to yours so you know what they are going for.

3 Fix whatever needs to be fixed prior to selling. This will help you sell your car for more money.

4 To advertise, run an ad in a local paper or put a sign on the car that it is for sale. Drive it around or park it in a place where a lot of people will see it. (Make sure the car is clean first!)

5 Mention to potential buyers that you did regular maintenance. If you have the service history, be sure to provide it.

INSURANCE

How to Find a Good Insurance Company

> **Note:** Before you start looking for an insurance company, consult your local DMV website to find out the type of coverage you'll need.

• Ask your friends, family, and coworkers for suggestions.

• Check consumer magazines and websites (e.g., *Consumer Reports*).

• Get a few different quotes from different insurance companies and compare prices. Geico is a good place to start.

Committing to a Plan with a Company

1 Ask for the highest liability coverage. This will afford you the greatest amount of protection in the event of an accident.

2 Consider purchasing "umbrella insurance." This protects you above and beyond what is offered by your policy.

3 Make sure you know what your deductible is, and how the premium will change if you choose to lower your deductible.

4 Make sure you're comfortable with your insurance company and agent. Meet the person who will be your agent; speak to them and ask how long they have worked at the company. Ask for a reference from another client and ask the reference how easily and efficiently their claims have been processed.

5 Ways to get a better deal:

Age-related discounts: If you are over fifty or retired, you might qualify.

Consolidate companies: Buy your home owner's insurance and car insurance from the same company.

Credit rating: If you have a good credit rating, tell the insurance company. You could get a better rate.

Group insurance: Ask whether you can purchase group insurance. You might be able to get this through your employer or through a professional or affiliate organization.

Higher deductible: Ask for a higher deductible. This could lower your premiums by 5 to 10 percent.

Low-mileage discounts: If you don't drive a lot, you might be eligible for a low-mileage discount.

Safe driver discounts: If you have a good driving record and have not had any accidents in a long time.

Safety records: Consider buying a car from a manufacturer that has a good safety record (for example, Volvo). This could lead to lower insurance costs.

Special safety features: Tell the insurance broker if you have air bags, antilock brakes, and/or antitheft devices in your car. Insurance companies give discounts for certain safety features.

MAINTENANCE CHECKLIST

EVERY THREE MONTHS OR EVERY 3,000 MILES

Change oil and filter.

Check all fluids.

Check hoses and belts.

Check tire pressure.

Lubricate chassis.

EVERY YEAR OR EVERY 10,000 MILES

Change brake fluid.

Change power steering fluid.

Check all ball joints.

Check all belts (including timing).

Check brakes and wheel bearings.

Check exhaust for any cracks and leaks.

Check for leaks.

Check temperature for engine thermostat.

Grease all door joints with liquid silicone.

Inspect cooling system, hoses, and fluid.

Replace all filters (PCV, air, fuel).

Replace all wipers.

Replace cap, rotor (all emissions items).

Rotate tires.

Align wheels.

EVERY TWO YEARS OR EVERY 20,000 MILES

Do everything listed in above checklist for 10,000 miles plus:

Change filter and clean screen and magnets.

Check all bulbs (headlights, blinkers, et cetera).

Check fuse panel.

Check operation of seats and sunroof (and grease them).

Check seals and door hinges.

Check the windshield for pitting and cracking.

Check tire wear and tear (replace tires if necessary).

Consider having undercarriage coated to prevent rusting if you live in a cold climate.

Drain, flush, and replace necessary fluids in cooling systems, radiator, engine block, and all heater-related components.

Renew brake fluid.

Replace automatic transmission fluid.

Update new navigation DVD.

EVERY THREE YEARS OR EVERY 30,000 MILES

Do everything listed in 10,000 miles checklist plus:

Car inspection.

Check and adjust pocket-style valves.

Check seat belts.

Check shocks.

Check undercarriage for rust (especially if you live in colder climates).

Check valve cover.

Have brake lines inspected.

Register car.

EVERY FIVE YEARS OR EVERY 50,000 MILES

Do everything listed in 10,000 miles checklist plus:

Change battery.

Check body bushings.

Check body surface (if there are any deep scratches that have not been treated, your car will start to rust).

Check door hinges.

Check exhaust.

Check motor and transmission mounts.

Replace oil in differentials and transfer case.

Replace oil in transmission.

Replace rubber timing belts on cam-shafts.

Check seat and seat belt operation.

EMERGENCY ITEMS TO KEEP IN YOUR CAR

12-foot jumper cables

30-minute high-intensity light stick

Adjustable wrench

Auto spotlight

Blanket

Bottled water

Duct tape

Energy bars

Extra fuses

Fire extinguisher

First-aid kit and medical supplies for any special medical needs in the family

Flashlight and extra batteries

Flat-head screwdriver

Four 15-minute roadside flares

Gallon of antifreeze

Ice scraper

Paper towels

Pen and paper

Phillips-head screwdriver

Pliers

Pocketknife

Rags

Rain poncho

Reflecting triangle

Special items for kids: diapers, toys, non-perishable snacks

Spray bottle with washer fluid

Tire inflator (such as a Fix-a-Flat)

Tire pressure gauge

Toilet paper

Tow rope

Two quarts of oil

Vise grips

Wet Naps

Instructions for any of the items above you wouldn't know how to use during an emergency

RESOURCES

MAGAZINES

Automobile

Car and Driver

Motor Trend

WEBSITES

autotrader.com

cars.com

edmunds.com

Kelley Blue Book: kbb.com

MEDICAL

Nowadays, surviving a hospital stay or even navigating through a protocol of preventative medical care can be a nerve-racking odyssey. But armed with a little bit of information in advance, you can have a relatively comfortable and low-stress trip to the doctor or even a relatively pleasant stay in the hospital.

Think you're pretty savvy already? Well, take this little quiz and find out: Do you keep a folder with all your medical records, X-rays, test results, and pharmacological history? If you have to go to the hospital for a stay, do you know what to pack? Is your medicine cabinet properly stocked, so if you get sick in the middle of the night you are not driving around bleary eyed at 1:30 a.m. looking for a pharmacy that's still open? If these questions have you breaking out in hives, don't worry. I'll provide you with all the information you'll need to clear those up and much more in the following chapter.

MEDICAL INSURANCE

Having medical insurance is imperative, but selecting a plan can be a daunting process. If you work for a company that offers health plans, your options have been narrowed down a bit for you. If you are employed, discuss your options with your human resources representative. But if you are paying for your own health insurance, choosing the right one can be confusing. Let me keep you from pulling your hair out.

Bear in mind that usually the more expensive plans will give you the least headaches. You need to select a plan that fits your budget, but you may feel it's worth investing in one that also affords you the flexibility to select doctors you prefer. In addition, there are some markets where many doctors take no insurance at all. Many insurance companies have websites that provide extensive information, so I'm not going to go into too much detail about each plan, but the most popular options for plans include PPO (Preferred Provider Organization), POS (Point of Service), and HMO (Health Maintenance Organization). The biggest differences in these plans have to do with the way you are able to select a doctor. The best advice I can offer is this: Do your homework and don't be afraid to ask questions.

What Am I Looking For?

Consider the following factors as you narrow your search:

1 Do I need single, couple, or family coverage?

2 What are my copay amounts to doctors?

3 What is my yearly deductible before I get re-imbursements or coverage?

4 What's my prescription coverage and what are my prescription deductibles?

5 What's my ER and hospital coverage?

6 Does the company have a website where I can research in-network doctors?

7 Can I also get dental and vision coverage?

8 Can I get mental health coverage?

9 What if I need rehabilitation?

10 Will the plan include maternity coverage?

Things to Do Once You Have Signed Up for a Plan

1 Keep a list of your in-network doctors in a safe place.

2 Make a copy of your insurance card and keep it with your important documents.

3 Always carry your card with you and bring it to the doctor's office, lab, hospital, or pharmacy—any place you may receive care.

4 Keep your doctors and pharmacies aware of new insurance cards or any changes in coverage.

5 Make sure your insurance company is aware of any changes regarding the name, address, and phone number of your primary physician.

6 Tell your insurance company of any changes to your name, address, phone number, marital status, of the birth or death of covered family members, or of a change of employer.

Pharmacies

Whenever possible, use a pharmacy that accepts your insurance and submits your claims.

ITEMS TO HAVE ON HAND AT HOME

MEDICINE CABINET AND MEDICAL SUPPLIES

Acidophilus

Aleve

Aloe vera gel

Aspirin

Bacitracin

Band-Aids

Benadryl

Blood pressure monitor

Caladryl

Calamine lotion

Chloraseptic spray

Cotton balls

Gauze pads

Hand sanitizer

Heating pads

Hydrogen peroxide

Ice packs

Imodium AD

Milk of magnesia

Motrin

Neosporin

Pepto-Bismol

Rubbing alcohol

Thermometer

Thermophore heating pad (see heating pad.com)

Tums (or any type of antacid you like)

Tweezers (Tweezerman is the best)

Tylenol

Vaseline

Visine

First-Aid Kit (should include: Band-Aid adhesive bandages, antiseptic wipes, Tylenol Extra Strength caplets, first-aid nonstick pads, Band-Aid antibiotic ointment with pain relief, burn cream, oval eye pads, nonlatex gloves, Kling gauze, elastic bandage, instant cold pack, first-aid tape, scissors, tweezers, and first-aid guide)

KIDS' MEDICINES TO KEEP ON HAND

Children's Benadryl

Children's Motrin

Children's Tylenol

Pedialyte

Important to Know: All medicines, vitamins, and supplements should be stored in a locked cabinet if there are young children in the home. Bear in mind that if you are taking prescription medications, you should consult your doctor before taking any of the above (as well as any other over-the-counter drugs and supplements).

TO-DOS FOR MAINTAINING YOUR HEALTH

This chart was adapted from a chart originally created by the South Carolina Medical Association in August 2006. It has been modified and is used with permission.

AGE	FEMALE and MALE
Newborn to 12 months **All Steps** newborn 2–4 days 1 month 2 months 4 months 6 months 9 months 12 months	developmental/behavioral assessment head circumference height and weight immunization physical examination anticipatory guidance: injury prevention nutrition counseling sleep positioning counseling (newborn to 6 months) violence prevention
Newborn or 2–4 days	hearing test hereditary/metabolic screening
Subjective, by history, or at risk	hematocrit or hemoglobin, 9–12 months lead screening, 9–12 months tuberculin test, 12 months (at risk) dental referral (at risk) vision test
15 months to 4 years **All Steps** 15 months 18 months 24 months 3 years 4 years	developmental/behavioral assessment head circumference (15–14 months) height and weight immunization physical examination anticipatory guidance: injury prevention nutrition counseling violence prevention
Subjective, by history, or at risk	cholesterol screening, all steps, if at risk hematocrit, 15 months or any age, if at risk tuberculin test, all steps, if at risk vision test, 15–24 months
24 months	lead screening, if at risk

AGE	FEMALE and MALE
3 years	vision test blood pressure dental referral, or any age after 12 months if indicated
4 years	hearing test, after that, as indicated vision test

5 years to 10 years
All steps
  5 years
  6 years
  8 years
  10 years
	developmental/behavioral assessment
	blood pressure
	head circumference
	hearing test
	height and weight
	immunization
	physical examination
	anticipatory guidance:
	  injury prevention
	  nutrition counseling
	  violence prevention

Subjective, by history, or at risk	cholesterol screening, all steps tuberculin test, all steps
5 years	urinalysis

11 to 18 years
annually
	developmental/behavioral assessment
	blood pressure
	hearing test
	height and weight
	immunization
	physical examination
	anticipatory guidance:
	  injury prevention
	  nutrition counseling
	  violence prevention

AGE	FEMALE	MALE
Subjective, by history, or at risk	cholesterol screening pelvic exam STD screening tuberculin test	

12 years, 15 years, 18 years	hearing test, or as
	   indicated
	vision test, or as
	   indicated	

13 years	hematocrit or
	   hemoglobin, or as
	   indicated	

16 years	urinalysis, or as indicated	
18 to 34 years annually	yearly physical blood pressure complete blood count STD tests breast exam pelvic exam Pap smear	yearly physical blood pressure complete blood count STD tests testicular self-exam
Subjective, by history, or at risk	**hepatitis immunization** **influenza immunization** mammogram rectal examination urinalysis	**hepatitis immunization** **influenza immunization** rectal examination urinalysis
Every 5 years	hemoglobin serum cholesterol	hemoglobin serum cholesterol

Every 10 years, or as indicated	booster shots for
	   tetanus, diphtheria,
	   and whooping cough
	   (pertussis) vaccines
		booster shots for
		   tetanus, diphtheria,
		   and whooping cough
		   (pertussis) vaccines

35 to 49 years annually	yearly physical
	blood pressure
	BMI
	complete blood count
	eye exam for glaucoma
	eye exam for vision
	fasting blood-glucose
	   test
	nonfasting total blood
	   cholesterol
	STD tests
	breast exam
	pelvic exam
	Pap smear
	mammogram
		yearly physical
		blood pressure
		BMI
		complete blood count
		eye exam for glaucoma
		eye exam for vision
		fasting blood-glucose
		   test
		nonfasting total blood
		   cholesterol
		STD tests
		testicular self-exam

MEDICAL

AGE	FEMALE	MALE
Subjective, by history, or at risk	**hepatitis immunization** **influenza immunization** rectal examination urinalysis	**hepatitis immunization** **influenza immunization** rectal examination urinalysis
Every 5 years, or as indicated	hemoglobin serum cholesterol thyroid screening	hemoglobin serum cholesterol
Every 10 years, or as indicated	booster shots for tetanus, diptheria, and whooping cough (pertussis) vaccines	booster shots for tetanus, diptheria, and whooping cough (pertussis) vaccines
50 to 64 years annually	yearly physical blood pressure BMI complete blood count colonoscopy, flexible sigmoidoscopy, or barium enema (ask doctor) eye exam for glaucoma eye exam for vision fasting blood-glucose test fecal occult blood test nonfasting total blood cholesterol STD tests breast exam pelvic exam Pap smear mammogram	yearly physical blood pressure BMI complete blood count colonoscopy, flexible sigmoidoscopy, or barium enema (ask doctor) eye exam for glaucoma eye exam for vision fasting blood-glucose test fecal occult blood test nonfasting total blood cholesterol STD tests testicular self-exam PSA screening
Subjective, by history, or at risk	**hepatitis immunization** **influenza immunization** rectal examination urinalysis	**hepatitis immunization** **influenza immunization** rectal examination urinalysis
Every 5 years, or as indicated	hemoglobin serum cholesterol thyroid screening	hemoglobin serum cholesterol
Every 10 years, or as indicated	booster shots for tetanus, diphtheria, and whooping cough (pertussis) vaccines	booster shots for tetanus, diphtheria, and whooping cough (pertussis) vaccines

AGE	FEMALE	MALE
65+ years, annually	yearly physical Alzheimer's screening blood pressure BMI colonoscopy, flexible sigmoidoscopy, or barium enema (ask doctor) complete blood count dual-energy X-ray absorptiometry DXA ear exam eye exam for glaucoma eye exam for vision fasting blood-glucose test fecal occult blood test nonfasting total blood cholesterol STD tests TSH blood test breast exam pelvic exam Pap smear mammogram	yearly physical Alzheimer's screening blood pressure BMI colonoscopy, flexible sigmoidoscopy, or barium enema (ask doctor) complete blood count dual-energy X-ray absorptiometry DXA ear exam eye exam for glaucoma eye exam for vision fasting blood-glucose test fecal occult blood test nonfasting total blood cholesterol STD tests TSH blood test AAA ultrasound testicular self-exam PSA screening
Subjective, by history, or at risk	**hepatitis immunization** **influenza immunization** rectal examination urinalysis	**hepatitis immunization** **influenza immunization** rectal examination urinalysis
Every 5 years, or as indicated	hemoglobin serum cholesterol thyroid screening	hemoglobin serum cholesterol
Every 10 years, or as indicated	booster shots for tetanus, diphtheria, and whooping cough (pertussis) vaccines	booster shots for tetanus, diphtheria, and whooping cough (pertussis) vaccines

MEDICAL

VISITING THE DOCTOR

Information to Have with You if You Are Ill and Seeking Treatment

1 Timeline of the current illness including pertinent medications, allergies, lab tests, and family history.

2 Answers to the following questions the doctor will ask:

Why are you here?

What are your symptoms?

What symptom is the most painful/bothersome? (Get to the point and skip the backstory.)

How long have you had these symptoms?

Do you have a family history of this condition?

3 Medical history:

All medications you are currently taking (name of drug and dosage). This list should include over-the-counter drugs as well as prescription drugs, and nutritional supplements, herbs and so on.

Any medical problems

Family illnesses

Past surgeries (type of surgery, date, results)

Current health conditions

Allergies

Things to Bring When You Return for a Diagnosis

1 Medical journal where you will keep all information. Write down *everything* the doctor says.

2 List of questions you want to ask (see below for examples).

3 A friend or family member to hear what the doctor says in case you miss something.

Questions to Ask Your Doctor

Remember to prioritize your questions. Ask the most important first, as your time with the doctor will be limited.

1 What is the diagnosis? How do you spell it?

2 How long is it medically safe to remain untreated?

3 Is there any recommended reading about the diagnosis I should check out?

4 Can you give me details about the treatment(s)?

5 Is there any recommended reading about the treatment(s)?

6 How can I contact you between now and my next visit? Do you use email?

7 Can I have a copy of all medical records, including doctor's notes and X-rays? (This saves time when you go for a second opinion.)

Note: Begin seeking recommendations for doctors to see for a second opinion soon after receiving the initial diagnosis.

Questions About Treatment

1 What are all of the treatment options?

2 How long will the treatment or surgery take?

3 What is the recovery time?

4 When can I go back to work?

5 Are there any side effects? How are they managed?

6 Is there a special diet that will need to be followed or dietary restrictions?

7 Do I need to fast prior to surgery? If so, are there any special instructions regarding fasting?

8 Are there any physical limitations?

9 Are there any medications that I should not be taking prior to surgery?

10 Any other special instructions?

HOSPITAL STAYS

General To-Dos

1 If possible, ask a friend or family member to make arrangements for food (lunch and dinner) to be brought to the hospital every day (also paper plates and utensils). This will be helpful for visitors or caretakers for the first few days. When you are feeling better, be sure to check with the doctor to see what food restrictions you may have.

2 Get a detailed list of instructions (any pre- or postoperation medical information you would need to know). Make copies.

3 Type up a list of your doctors' phone numbers. Include doctors who are not directly involved in the current procedure in case they need to be consulted.

4 Make all necessary insurance arrangements. Confirm that your doctor and/or the hospital have received all insurance company approvals.

5 Schedule the surgery for a day that is convenient, if possible.

6 Avoid holiday admissions, and know that June and July mark the official beginning of most hospital rotations, so the staff doctors can be new. Take extra care during this time.

7 Type up a list of your medications or special needs.

8 Have previous lab results or films ready and on hand.

9 Prepare a power of attorney and a living will. Be sure doctors are aware of these, and copies are in your file.

Day Before To-Dos

1 Pack bags (see page 202).

2 Charge cell phones, BlackBerry, PDA, iPod.

3 Prepare food for the next day.

4 Take off all your jewelry, including wedding bands, and leave them where they'll be safe—home.

5 Review procedure instructions (preparations for the surgery and anything for post-op).

6 Review the list of doctors you have typed up to double-check that all phone numbers are correct.

7 Print out exact directions of how to get to the hospital, if needed.

Day of To-Dos

1 Have someone on standby to run errands (for food, items accidentally left at home).

2 Follow any instructions from the doctor.

3 Double-check that you have all your medical information packed, as well as contact lists.

ADVICE FOR FRIENDS, FAMILY, AND CAREGIVERS

- Friends should offer to come by to visit every day (if not for the patient, then for the person taking care of the patient to have a break). Do not bring children unless the patient specifically asks you to and the hospital permits.
- Good gifts to send to the hospital include:
Food (this is the best gift. No one has time to leave the hospital to get food, and hospital food isn't great).
Flowers and balloons are good gifts, too, but note that some hospitals will not allow them, so be sure to double-check before sending.
- Talk softly whenever you are in the room. Realize the patient may not want you there at all, but know that showing up is really important.
- If you are taking care of someone in the hospital, try to take a shower when the patient is sleeping.
- Do not give out the room phone number to anyone. Call people only on cell phones, or pay phones if cell phones are not allowed. Otherwise the room phone will be ringing nonstop.

(You can't turn off the ringer in a hospital, but you can request the operator to stop all calls.)

- Everything that you bring or send to the hospital should be immediately washed or dry-cleaned when you get home to prevent spread of hospital-borne infections.
- Keep all get well cards and remember to send thank-you notes to everyone who sends a gift.
- Keep bags packed until the patient is completely better in case you have to go back to the hospital.

HOSPITAL PACKING LIST
(FOR A ONE-WEEK STAY)

Baby wipes (entire box)

Bathrobe, cotton (2)

Bathing suit or T-shirt and shorts in case you need to take a shower in front of someone and you feel shy about them seeing you undressed

Blankets (3). It's always freezing in the hospital, and when they take you for tests you always want to have an extra blanket with you.

Cash ($200)

Clock (battery operated)

Clothes for leaving the hospital

Copy of this list

Copy of your living will and health care proxy

DVD player, adapter, battery

Earplugs (your neighbor can be noisy)

Eye shades or mask

Flashlights

Flip-flops (standing in the shower can be gross)

Gum or mints. Sometimes you have bad breath but don't want to get out of bed to brush your teeth.

Hand sanitizer for room and bathroom

Headphones

Insurance card and a copy of insurance card

iPod and speakers for iPod

List of medications

List of people to call in case of an emergency and their phone numbers

List of important doctors and their contact info

Magazines and other reading materials

Medications (bring your own medications in the event the hospital does not have exactly what you need in stock)

Mouthwash

Movies for the DVD player

Pajamas

Paper and pen

Phone and charger

Pictures of family

Pillows and colored pillowcases (so they don't get mixed up with hospital linens)

Quarters for pay phones in case your cell phone isn't working

Shopping bags (you are always taking things to and from the hospital)

Sign for the door that says "Do Not Enter—Please Knock and Talk Softly" and tape

Slippers

Snacks and drinks for visitors

Socks (6 pairs)

Surgery list (history of surgery)

Sweatpants

Thermometer (digital)

Tissues (box)

Toilet paper (yours is probably much softer than what the hospital will provide)

Toiletry bag for travel

Toothpaste, toothbrush, dental floss

Towels

T-shirts (white cotton)

Underwear

Wallet with cash, credit card, and card listing important phone numbers

Water

Once You Are in the Hospital: Advice for the Patient

1 Get to know team members fast. Know the difference between your internist, specialist, resident, intern, surgeon, partners, covering physician, nurse, therapists, and anyone else of importance. Tip: Bring a gift of some kind for the nurses (for example, cookies). This small gesture will go a long way.

2 Know who the lead physician is; he makes the decisions.

3 Don't be shy. Ask questions. Take notes. Studies show this can make the difference between success and failure, or life and death.

4 If you share a room with someone, introduce yourself.

5 Sometimes you may get a "bad neighbor," who is loud, very sick, or has a lot of visitors. If this happens, request a room change. Be considerate of others for the same reason.

6 Know where your best veins are. If you are a difficult stick, request only a phlebotomist. Someone with poor blood drawing skills can ruin your stay in a matter of minutes. Post a note above your bed that says "Best vein in left antecubital area" or "Do not use left arm for blood draw."

MEDICAL

Advice for the Patient Advocate

1 If your friend or family member suffers from nausea, be careful of offensive odors. If they have respiratory problems, try not to use perfumes or strong-smelling soaps.

2 Get friends and family members involved if you need coverage. Anything that can go wrong will go wrong in the hospital. The more eyes and ears, the better. As a rule, someone should be with the patient at all times. This rule becomes more rigid the sicker the patient is. Think about hiring an aide or private nurse.

3 Encourage the patient, hold her hand, talk to her. Morale is critical to recovery.

4 Know which drugs the patient is taking (e.g., thyroid medication, antidepressants, blood pressure medication, asthma medications). Not communicating or being aware of this information can have serious and even life-threatening consequences.

5 Wash your hands or use Purell before entering or leaving the hospital.

6 Every time you see the doctor, ask when they are coming back again. You don't want to be having to chase the doctor down.

Day Before Discharge To-Dos

1 Have your doctor write—legibly—all necessary prescriptions you will need and review how to take them.

2 Arrange transportation home.

3 Ask you doctor when he wants to see you next after you leave the hospital.

4 Ask you doctor what follow-up treatments will be required. For example, will you need physical therapy? If so, who does he recommend and when should you start?

5 Ask your doctor about the best way to reach him should you have any problems when you leave the hospital.

6 Read any special instructions that your doctor has given you and ask him questions.

7 Be sure your doctor has the discharge order ready.

RESOURCES

BOOKS

The Merck Manual of Medical Information, 2nd Home Edition, by Mark H. Beers

Physicians' Desk Reference

MAGAZINES

Prevention

Self

WEBSITES

Agency for Healthcare Research and Quality (ARHQ): ahrq.gov/consumer/surgery/surgery.htm

American Medical Association: ama-assn.org

Consumer and Patient Health Information Section (CAPHIS): caphis.mlanet.org/consumer (lists top 100 sites "you can trust." This site is great since it discusses each site's strength and breaks them down into categories such as general, women, men, et cetera.)

eMedicine: emedicine.medscape.com

eBizMBA: ebizmba.com/articles/health (tracks the top twenty health-related sites by hits)

Health Central: healthcentral.com

iVillage: ivillage.com

Mayo Clinic: mayoclinic.com

Medicine Net: medicinenet.com

Medscape: medscape.com

Mercksource: mercksource.com

National Jewish Health: nationaljewish.org/healthinfo/index.aspx

Strength For Caring: strengthforcaring.com

National Family Caregivers Association: www.thefamilycaregiver.org

UCSF Health (University of California, San Francisco: ucsfhealth.org/adult/edu/communicatingwithyourdoctor.html

WebMD: webMD.com

Important to note: Do not draw any conclusions on your own. Review the information you read on the sites and discuss your findings with your doctor for a proper diagnosis.

DIVORCE

Who knew that getting out of a marriage would be so much harder than getting into one? Almost 50 percent all of marriages in the United States end in divorce.

If you find, however, that you have to say "I don't," it's important to be prepared not only emotionally and mentally, but also fiscally. When the time comes you must be armed with as much personal and financial documentation that you can gather—your *own* and your spouse's. Gathering all of this information will be necessary to your lawyer, and having it already compiled by the time you meet will save you time and money in attorney's fees, which will quickly add up.

While going through a divorce is never easy, I hope these lists will make the process go a bit more smoothly.

What Your Attorney Will Need to Know

- Assets: What assets do you and your spouse own? Cars, art, jewelry, household furnishings.

- Statements for the past three years for *all* bank accounts held, either individually or jointly

- Investments: Account statements for stocks, bonds, mutual funds, retirement funds, and any other investments

- Bills paid online: Tell your attorney whether you know the user name and password for each account.

- Children's needs: Current and future needs of the minor children of the marriage. Include food, clothing, medical, current education, insurance, child care, necessary travel expenses, transportation, entertainment, haircuts, gifts, holidays, higher education.

- Conduct: When did you stop being married and why?

- Contributions of each party in the acquisition and preservation in the value of the estate

- Credit histories: Try to provide a copy of Equifax, Experian, and TransUnion credit histories for you and your spouse.

- Debts: How much money do you owe? Are there any liabilities? Are you paying off your student loans? How much are the mortgage and your expenses? What have you both run up on those charge cards?

- Employability: If either of you is out of work, can you get a job?

- Estate-planning documents: Copy of your will, your spouse's will, and any other estate-planning documents, such as a living trust agreement

- Estates: What does each of you own?

- Financial overview: An overview of your financial situation

- Financial statements: Copies of any financial statements prepared separately or together when you applied for a loan

- Future income: What opportunities does each of you have for future income?

- Home loans or lines of credit

- Insurance policies: Copies of all life insurance policies that list you or your spouse as the owner or beneficiary

- Length of marriage

- Living expenses: Monthly living expenses

- Loans: Copy of any loan or mortgage applications made within the last three years prior to filing for divorce

- Marriage certificate: Certified copy of your marriage certificate (write to the city where you were married)

- Money: Amounts and sources of income, everything you both earn and everything you each are hiding

- Needs of the respective parties. Remember, "need" is a very subjective term. Separate your needs from your wants. Food is a need. Lavish vacations are wants.

- Occupations of the respective parties

- Ownership papers for your assets and approximate values of each

- P&L statements: If you own a business, provide your attorney with profit and loss statements and balance sheets and copies of related partnerships, agreements, or articles of incorporation.

- Pay stubs: The four most recent pay stubs for each employer

- Personal, car, student, or business loans

- Prenups: Copies of any prenuptial or postnuptial agreements

- Professional contacts: names and contact info for your accountants, bankers, attorneys, financial advisers, stockbrokers

- Real estate tax bills for the current year

- Social Security numbers and salary information

- Tax returns for any nonpublic, limited partnership, and privately held corporate returns for any entity in which either party has an interest

- Individual and joint tax returns for the past five years (visit www.irs.ustreas.gov)

Questions to Ask Your Attorney

1 How long have you been practicing divorce law, and what percentage of your law practice is divorce cases?

2 How many cases have you handled, and how many have gone to trial?

3 If my divorce goes to trial, will you or your associate represent me?

4 How much is your retainer, and under what circumstances is the retainer refundable?

5 What are your hourly rates, and are they subject to change? What about rates for associates, for administrative work? Consultation rates? Estimated expenses?

6 How do you calculate your billable hours? Are there minimum billing increments? For example, if we talk for five minutes, are you going to bill me for fifteen minutes? (Remember, every minute you talk to your attorney is billable time.)

7 What can I do to minimize my legal expenses?

8 Will your billing rate go up after one year? (Ask this before you sign a retainer in order to keep your billing rates the same for the length of your case.)

9 Will I receive monthly itemized statements?

Personal Safeguard To-Dos

• Appraisals: Have all your jewelry appraised and insured.

• Bank account: Open a bank account in your own name.

• Billing addresses: Change billing address to a parent, sibling, or post office box for all your financial statements (bank accounts, credit cards, cell phone, BlackBerry).

- Cash: Save, save, save. Stash your cash. Put it in a safety deposit box, as your bank accounts may be frozen.

- Cell phone: Get a new cell phone so you can communicate with your lawyer and friends privately.

- Children: Notify your children's teachers, coaches, and other adult mentors about your pending divorce. Ask them to notify you of any changes in your child's behavior.

- Credit cards: Cancel joint credit cards.

- Credit history: Build a good credit history in your own name (and clean up a bad one if you have it).

- Debts: Clear up any outstanding debts in either/both of your names. Perhaps pay off that car lease!

- Doctor appointments: Take care of any doctor appointments that need to be done before you initiate the divorce (for example, dentist, eye doctor, plastic surgery).

- Email: Set up a new email address for divorce-related communications only. Set up a second one for friends and family you trust, but keep divorce discussions to a minimum. And do not share your password with anyone.

- Fun: Do something you've always wanted to do (take a painting or dance class).

- Health care proxy: Change health care proxy and living will.

- Inheritances: Have any potential inheritance placed in a trust for you.

- Journal: Keep a diary of activities and time spent with your children. Best to be in Super Mom or Super Dad mode in the event of a custody dispute. Also include all negative events involving you or your children (physical or verbal abuse). If you have a witness, have her sign the journal.

- Monthly expenses: Put together a budget of your monthly expenses.

- New home: Think about where you will be living if your home is going to be sold.

- Ownership papers: Locate ownership papers for all your assets.

- Passports: Remove your and your children's passports from the house. Put them in a safe place.

- Photos: Make copies of photos or photo albums you will want.

- Safe deposit box: Purchase or rent a bank safe deposit box and cosign with a family member or trusted friend. Do not open one in your own name. Place important documents, jewelry, and other valuables there for protection.

- Security: Change all passwords and codes (voicemail, email, bank accounts, credit cards, social networking sites, et cetera).

- Therapist: Find a couples' therapist or marriage counselor to help you navigate the divorce process.

- Valuables: Remove anything you consider valuable (jewelry, family heirlooms, clothing, photo albums) from your home as early as possible.

- Will: Change your will to accommodate your impending change in marital status.

DIVORCE

Put Money Aside For

- A retainer for your attorney. Ask your attorney for an estimate of your costs and the time the process is expected to take.

- One year's rent for an apartment or home.

- Money to live on for six months in the event your credit cards and bank accounts are closed by your spouse.

RESOURCES

BOOKS

Dinosaurs Divorce: A Guide for Changing Families, by Laurence Krasny Brown and Marc Brown

The Fresh Start Divorce Recovery Workbook: A Step-by-Step Program for Those Who Are Divorced or Separated, by Bob Burns and Tom Whiteman

Healing the Wounds of Divorce: A Spiritual Guide to Recovery, by Barbara Leahy Shlemon

I Don't Want to Talk About It, by Jeanie Franz Ransom

It Happens Every Day, by Isabel Gillies

It's Not Your Fault, Koko Bear: A Read-Together Book for Parents & Young Children During Divorce, by Vicki Lansky

Let's Talk About It: Divorce, by Fred Rogers

Mama and Daddy Bear's Divorce, by Cornelia Maude Spelman

Mom's House, Dad's House: Making Two Homes for Your Child, by Isolina Ricci

What About the Kids? Raising Your Children Before, During, and After Divorce, by Judith S. Wallerstein and Sandra Blakeslee

Your Kids and Divorce: Helping Them Grow Beyond the Hurt, by Thomas A. Whiteman

WEBSITES

Divorce Central: divorcecentral.com

Divorce Doctor: divorcedoctor.com

Divorce Helpline: divorcehelp.com

Divorceinfo: divorceinfo.com

DivorceNet: divorcenet.com

Divorce Online: divorceonline.com

Divorce Source: divorcesource.com

Divorce Wizards: divorcewizards.com

Flying Solo: flyingsolo.com

Woman's Divorce: womansdivorce.com

A Kid's Guide to Divorce: kidshealth.org/kid/feeling/home_family/divorce.html

Kids' Turn Central: kidsturncentral.com/topics/issues/divorce.htm

POSTMORTEM

No matter how much advance notice you may have had, nothing prepares you emotionally for the loss of a loved one. I will leave that chapter to the therapists and grief counselors, but what I can do is guide you, step by step, through the administrative process that accompanies the end of life's journey.

If you have just lost someone dear, the only thing you want to do is give or get support from family and friends. If the responsibility of planning the funeral lands in your lap, you might have to deal with everything from the Social Security Administration to the Department of Motor Vehicles, as well as the more immediate tasks of choosing a casket, writing the obituary, and planning the service.

The best advice I can offer is to use this chapter as a guide to creating your own "End of Life" folder of documents, special instructions, and information. When the time comes, your family will be comforted by your having had everything assembled in advance.

Immediate To-Dos

You will need this information about the deceased to tie up their affairs and plan the funeral.

- Family doctor name and number
- Estate lawyer name and number
- Location of will
- Social Security number
- Mother's maiden name
- Address
- Date of birth
- Place of birth
- Father's name
- Proof of military service (when applicable)
- Date, place, cause of death
- Occupation and date last worked
- List of people important to the deceased: closest friends, boss, their names and phone numbers
- Location of the family plot
- List of bank accounts, bank safe deposit boxes, and IRA account information
- Life insurance policies

Next Step To-Dos

1 Contact immediate family (your immediate family will want to hear from you personally in your own voice; no emails, please). If possi-

ble, have the date, time, and location of funeral/ service information handy. Most people will ask when you call. But chances are it will take you a few days to plan everything. However, don't wait until you have funeral details to make these calls—most people will want to know right away that the person has passed away.

2 Make a list of all the people (names *and* contact info) you don't want to call and have someone call them.

3 Choose a funeral home within twenty-four hours of the death. For a referral, consult your family, friends, rabbi, priest, family doctor, social worker at the hospital, or the yellow pages.

4 Get the funeral home to fill out a death certificate.

5 Get fifteen original/certified copies of the death certificate. You will need these copies in order to remove a name from a home or car title; joint bank and securities accounts; to collect life insurance proceeds; to obtain hospital records; to file a lawsuit; or anything else that might come up. If you need more copies, you may have to wait another month.

6 Get a letter from the funeral home to obtain bereavement fares on airlines for those who may need it.

7 Locate wills and other legal paperwork necessary for probate court. (The will states the deceased's wishes regarding services, burial, cremation.)

POSTMORTEM

8 Call the deceased's life insurance company representative as soon as possible to notify them of the death. This is important.

9 Write the obituary. This is timely because it needs to go in the paper the next day. (Note: Buy a newspaper and read how other obituaries were written.)

> Survived by (list all family members who you want listed who are still living).

> Make it clear where the deceased worked and went to school (e.g., went to Harvard University and worked at IBM for ten years).

> If you don't want people to send flowers, consider writing: "In lieu of flowers please send donations to deceased's favorite charity."

10 While many people will bring food to you, you might also want to have some additional easy-to-prepare food on hand so you don't have to rely on others. If you don't want to prepare it yourself, enlist a good friend or family member to help.

11 If the deceased had children or young relatives with whom he/she was close, notify the children's school.

12 Find photographs of the deceased (the funeral home and newspapers may need them).

13 Cancel the deceased's credit cards.

14 Close the deceased's bank accounts.

15 Notify the Department of Motor Vehicles if the deceased had a valid driver's license.

16 Contact the deceased's health insurance company. (Note: If you were married to the deceased and on your spouse's health insurance, you will have coverage for a limited time depending on the policy. After that time expires, you will need to find another health insurance plan).

17 Contact the Social Security Administration to obtain death benefits for the spouse and the children of the deceased (these do not automatically take effect, you must apply). Go to socialsecurity.gov or call 800-772-1213. To apply you will need:

> Death certificate (certified copy)
>
> Birth certificates of surviving spouse and children
>
> Bank account number that benefits should be deposited into
>
> Proof of marriage (a certified copy of the marriage certificate)
>
> Picture identification (yours)
>
> Proof of citizenship (yours)
>
> Record of the deceased's earnings in the year prior to death (W-2 form or tax return)
>
> Social Security numbers of the surviving spouse and children and the deceased

POSTMORTEM

Funerals: What to Send and Do

What to Send

1. Send a card with your loving thoughts and wishes.

> Suggestions

> "What we once enjoyed and deeply loved we can never lose, for all that we love deeply becomes a part of us." —Helen Keller

> Loving thoughts are with you.

2. Food

> Make food yourself and deliver it.

> Call a local restaurant and ask them to prepare meals.

> Look online for other delivery resources.

3. Flowers

> Send the flowers to the person's home as opposed to the funeral home (they often get overlooked or thrown out at the funeral home).

Note: Do not send flowers to a Jewish funeral or the home of a Jewish family. This is against Jewish custom.

4. Donation to charity

> Ask someone close to the family which charity was the deceased's favorite; if they don't have one, then choose one you think the deceased might have liked.

→

Make the donation directly to the organization and send a card to the family letting them know that a donation has been made in memory of the deceased.

Advice for Friends and Family

• If you feel it's appropriate, call and visit the deceased's loved ones and share your fond memories of the deceased. Do this as often as you think they'll appreciate it.

• Bring food as often and for as long as you can.

• Offer to watch the children.

• Offer help. Say, "I am here if you need anything," and follow up with phone calls often.

• Send a card or letter if you cannot attend the funeral or are not close enough with the family to call.

THE FUNERAL

Initial To-Dos

1 Determine who will pay for the funeral.

2 Select a funeral home. The funeral home will take care of the following:

Transporting the body to the place of the service

Planning the services. Note: They will try to sell you the most expensive version of everything. They are in the business of funerals. Don't feel pushed into spending anything you don't want to.

Helping you find someone to officiate at the service if you do not already have someone in mind.

Burial or cremation

3 Make a list of who to invite to the funeral. Once that's been determined, you can call people (and have friends help you call) with details. The funeral information will also appear in the obituary, if you have one in the newspaper.

4 People might ask you about a charity to which they can make donations in the deceased's name. Be prepared to supply names of charities and contact information.

5 Decide if and where you want to receive guests. Most people do so in their homes. Have someone arrange for food and beverages to be delivered to the reception location on the day of the service.

To-Dos for the Funeral Ceremony

1 Select music.

2 Provide photographs of the deceased to display.

3 Give or assign the eulogy: Generally, this is done by an immediate family member or close friend of the deceased.

4 Ask the funeral home about ordering a headstone. There are many styles to choose from, and the cemetery may have other specifications you must observe. Find out how long it takes to make. Figure out what you want written on the headstone. This is one of the more complicated to-dos that will take some time since what will be written will last forever. If the deceased's spouse is still alive and he or she so desires, you might consider leaving space on the stone if the two planned to be buried together.

5 Decide who you will ask to serve as pallbearers (you need at least six men).

6 Arrange for transportation of flowers out of the funeral home or church, as they will tell you they need to have them removed before the next event immediately following.

> Be sure to send acknowledgments for any gifts you receive. If necessary, assign this job to a friend so you can deal with more difficult tasks. Try to do this no longer than one month after the death.

After the Funeral: Legal Affairs To-Dos

1 If you are the spouse, locate your proof of marriage. Before you can inherit from the estate, existing policies, or investments, you will need to present an official marriage certificate. The website www.cdc.gov/nchs provides information on requesting certified copies of death and marriage certificates.

2 Open an estate bank account. It is important to do this instead of simply writing checks out of your own account. In the event a claim comes in against the deceased, you want it to go against the bank account and not the closest relative/wife.

3 Call the estate lawyer and the executor of the estate.

> Get the letters testamentary—a legal document you will need in order to open up a bank account for the estate.

> Have them file a closure of the estate in court. This is only done after a reasonable amount of time has passed and there are no claims for money against the estate. At that point, the executor is discharged from the estate, and the estate can be closed along with the bank account.

> Rerecord property deeds.

4 File an estate tax return.

RESOURCES

BOOKS

> *The Last Lecture*, by Randy Pausch

> *What Remains: A Memoir of Fate, Friendship, and Love*, by Carole Radziwill

> *When Bad Things Happen to Good People*, by Harold S. Kushner

> *The Year of Magical Thinking*, by Joan Didion

BOOKS FOR CHILDREN

Dog Heaven, by Cynthia Rylant

Goodbye Mousie, by Robie H. Harris and Jan Ormerod

Saying Goodbye to Daddy, by Judith Vigna

A Story for Hippo, by Simon Puttock and Alison Bartlett

What on Earth Do You Do When Someone Dies?, by Trevor Romain

When a Pet Dies, by Fred Rogers

EMERGENCY

One day a friend turned to me out of the blue and said, "Do you have an emergency plan for the family?" Even though I was in New York City on September 11, 2001, somehow I had never thought about having a plan in place should a catastrophe occur. So I put together this checklist. It is not meant to be used at the time of an emergency, but instead as an advance way to plan with the family (or at least educate the family about how to react). Please note that this is the plan I designed for my family that you can use as a basis for your own plan, along with information you can find on the websites of the Red Cross and FEMA.

DISASTER RECOVERY PLAN

My comprehensive Family Plan for disaster preparation, reaction, and recovery is composed of *two* parts: The first part details the Emergency Supply Kit, the Go Bag, and the First-Aid Kit contents. The second part lists possible threats/disasters and the methods of preparation, reaction, and recovery.

EMERGENCY BAGS AND KITS

Note: The First-Aid Kit is part of the Go Bag, and the Go Bag is a part of the Emergency Supply Kit.

First-Aid Kit

- A box of latex or other sterile gloves
- Sterile dressings to stop bleeding
- Cleansing agent/soap and antibiotic towelettes to disinfect
- Hydrogen peroxide
- Alcohol
- Iodine
- Betadene
- Acetaminophen, ibuprofen, aspirin, Aleve
- Antibiotic ointment
- Antidiarrheal
- Burn ointment
- Hydrocortisone cream
- Adhesive bandages in a variety of sizes
- Tourniquet
- Razor and blades
- Electrolyte solution
- Saline solution
- Elastic wrap
- Triangular bandages

- Scissors with rounded tips

- 2-inch gauze squares

- Disposable, instant ice bags

- Tweezers

- Safety pins

- Dust masks

- Eye wash solution to flush the eyes or as general decontaminant

- Prescription medications you take every day such as insulin, heart medicine, and asthma inhalers. Check regularly to discard and replace expired medications.

- Prescribed medical supplies such as glucose and blood pressure monitoring equipment

Emergency Go Bag

You can find lists for what to put in your Go Bag online at places such as www.72hours.org/index.html. My personal bag includes the following:

- First-Aid Kit

- Copies of important documents in a waterproof and portable container (insurance cards, photo IDs, proof of address, bank account records, et cetera)

- Extra set of car and house keys

- Credit and ATM cards and cash, especially in small denominations. You should have at least $50 to $100 on hand.

- Bottled water and nonperishable food such as energy or granola bars

- Flashlight (no battery required)

- Wind-up (no battery required) AM/FM/VHF "public alert" radio

- List of the medications each family member takes, why they take them, and their dosages; medication information and other essential personal items

- Plastic sheets and duct tape

- Thermals for entire family

- Mylar blankets

- Toilet paper

- Water purifying tablets

- Notebook and pencils

- Matches in a waterproof container

- Whistle

- Feminine hygiene supplies

- Contact and meeting place information for the family, and a small regional map

Emergency Supply Kit

My list includes:

- One gallon of drinking water per person per day for at least three days

- Nonperishable, ready-to-eat, and canned foods and manual can opener. I packed:

10 cans of corn, 10 cans of baked beans, 20 cans of tuna, 10 cans of sweet peas, 10 cans of corned beef, 3 jars of peanut butter, 30 servings of different kinds of "just add water" soup mixes, 10 packages of crackers, 6 packages of trail mix, and 20 juice boxes (for the kids)

- Phone that does not rely on electricity
- Emergency Go Bag (includes the First-Aid Kit).

HURRICANE

To-Dos Once a Hurricane Watch Has Been Issued

1 Monitor the local news for hurricane alerts.

2 Fill the gas tanks in all cars and get an extra five-gallon tank of gas for the evacuation car (preferably a vehicle that has four-wheel drive).

3 Put a package of twenty-four water bottles in the evacuation car.

4 Turn off propane tanks.

5 Bring all loose objects—including all outdoor furniture, barbecue, decorations, garbage cans, and anything else that is not tied down—in from outside.

6 Shut all windows and doors securely.

EMERGENCY

7 Remove art from walls and store it in a safe place. Make a list of your art in case it gets lost or damaged.

8 Unplug electrical appliances and move them to the upper level. Make a list of the appliances in case anything gets lost or damaged.

9 Move the cars into the garage and securely close the garage doors.

10 Lock the house and evacuate as soon as possible. Take the Go Bag in the evacuation car.

11 If there is no time to leave town, evacuate to the closest evacuation center (call the public safety line for details).

12 Call extended family members and let them know when you left, where you are headed, and when you arrive at the destination.

13 Listen to the news for advised travel routes. Do not try to find shortcuts!

14 Avoid flooded roadways. Parts of the road may already be washed out, and you could become stranded or trapped.

15 If the car stalls in a flooded area, abandon it as soon as possible. Floodwaters can rise rapidly and sweep a car (and its occupants) away.

EMERGENCY

Family To-Dos

1 Gather entire family in one location.

2 Prepare Go Bags.

3 Monitor the local news and follow instructions for evacuation.

4 Listen for announcements that your location is under evacuation orders or check online at: gis.nyc.gov/oem/he/index.htm

> or check by phone: [enter your local information number here]

5 If evacuating, take the Go Bag, located at
_____.

6 If decided to go to a "No Evacuation Zone" in town, the family will go to:

> 1st option: _____
>
> 2nd option: _____
>
> 3rd option: _____

If decided to go out of town, the family will go to:

> 1st option: _____
>
> 2nd option: _____
>
> 3rd option: _____

7 Once you are at the location, stay wherever you are until authorities say it is safe to go out. Stay as far away as possible from all windows.

EMERGENCY

REMINDERS AND FYIs

Hurricane season is June 1 through November 30.

Do not take shelter in the basement, which might get flooded. Evacuate instead.

If you're caught inside by rising waters:

Move to a higher floor.

Wait for help.

Do not touch an electric appliance if you are wet or standing in water.

Don't attempt to walk across stretches of floodwaters more than knee deep.

Don't try to swim to safety.

Pre-Hurricane

3 Months Before Hurricane Season

1 Inspect walls, windows, garage doors, and roof for conditions that may allow wind or water damage and have them repaired.

2 Make sure there are proper "check valves" installed to prevent floodwater from backing up into the drains.

3 Have all trees and shrubs trimmed.

Post-Hurricane

1 Do not enter the house until local officials confirm it is safe.

2 Do not enter the house before communicating with and receiving instructions from the insurance company.

3 Check with town hall for licensed post-storm contractors.

HEAT WAVE

To-Dos When the Temperature Is Rising

1 Keep the house cool.

2 Stay inside the house.

3 Avoid strenuous outdoor activities.

4 Drink plenty of water.

5 Eat light, well-balanced meals.

6 Dress in light, loose-fitting clothing.

7 Never leave children alone in a closed vehicle.

FYI: SIGNS OF DEHYDRATION

Dry, sticky mouth, thirst

Lack of sweating

Sleepiness or tiredness; children are likely to be less active than usual.

Irritability and confusion

Decreased urine output: Eight hours without urination; dark yellow or amber urine

Few or no tears when crying

Muscle weakness

Headache

Dizziness or lightheadedness

Sunken eyes

Shriveled and dry skin that lacks elasticity and doesn't "bounce back" when pinched into a fold

Low blood pressure

Rapid heartbeat

Fever

Preparing for the Heat

Two Months Before Summer (April 1)

1 Make sure the house cooling system is working properly.

2 Make sure the house is well insulated and that there is weather stripping around your doors and windowsills to keep the cool air inside.

EXTREME WINTER CONDITIONS

General Plan

1 Monitor the local news.

2 Have enough supplies on hand and plan to stay inside and make it on your own for at least three days.

3 Thoroughly check and update the family's Emergency Supply Kit before winter approaches (try to do this around October 1).

Buy and Store

This is my personal list. I recommend researching and creating your own personalized version.

• 24 gallons of water (1 gallon per day per person for 3 days for 8 people)

• Canned food and 3 manual can openers

    10 cans of corn

    10 cans of baked beans

    20 cans of tuna

    10 cans of sweet peas

10 cans of corned beef

3 jars of peanut butter

- 30 servings of different kinds of "just add water" soup mixes

- 10 packages of crackers (different brands)

- 6 packages of trail mix (nuts and dried fruit)

- 20 juice boxes (for the kids)

- Wood and burnable materials for the fireplace (in case of a power outage during a rough winter).

EARTHQUAKE

General Plan

1 Monitor the news. Bear in mind, smaller quakes and sometimes larger ones can often follow hours or days after the initial shake, causing further damage to weakened buildings and structures.

2 Take cover under a sturdy piece of furniture, away from glass and anything that could fall.

3 Stay inside until the shaking stops, and when you leave the building, use the stairs, not the elevator.

4 If the family needs to get back together and local phones do not work, communicate through an out-of-town contact: _____.

REMINDERS AND FYIs

- Stay away from large windows, mirrors, or other glass.

- Do not leave the shelter right away; there might be immediate aftershocks.

- When outside, stay clear of buildings, building exits, exterior walls, power lines, overpasses, and elevated expressways.

- Do not return home until a licensed construction engineer has approved that the building is safe.

- Do not enter the house before communicating with the insurance company for instructions.

Yearly To-Dos

1 Make sure all shelves are securely fastened to walls.

2 Inspect and repair electrical wiring and gas connections; these can be potential fire hazards during an earthquake.

3 Secure the water heater by strapping it to wall studs and bolting it to the floor.

4 Check the house for structural defects and repair cracks in the ceiling and foundation.

EMERGENCY

After an Earthquake

1 Turn off the main gas, water, and electricity at the outside main valves.

2 If you hear a hissing or blowing noise, make sure the house has been evacuated and call the gas company.

FIRE

General Plan

1 Exit the building ASAP.

2 Listen for announcements and follow instructions.

3 Crawl low if there is smoke.

4 Cover your nose and mouth with a wet cloth to avoid inhaling the smoke.

5 Use the back of your hand to feel the upper, lower, and middle parts of closed doors.

If the door is not hot, brace yourself against it and open it slowly.

If the door is hot, do not open it. Look for another way out.

6 Take the stairs to the exit. Do not use elevators.

7 When you are safely outside the building, call 911.

IF YOU ARE TRAPPED IN DEBRIS

Avoid unnecessary movement so that you don't kick up dust.

Cover your nose and mouth with anything you have on hand. (Dense-weave cotton material can act as a good filter. Try to breathe through the material.)

Tap on a pipe or wall so that rescuers can hear where you are.

Shout only as a last resort. Shouting can cause a person to inhale dangerous amounts of dust.

REMINDERS AND FYIs

If you catch on fire, do not run. Stop, drop, and roll to put out the fire.

Never go back into a burning building.

Do not enter the house until local officials confirm it is safe.

Do not enter the house before communicating with the insurance company for instructions.

NEED TO KNOW

The nearest emergency exit is located

_____.

The fire extinguisher is located _____

_____.

EMERGENCY

BOMB, CRASH, EXPLOSION

While Inside a Building

1 Move away from file cabinets, bookshelves, or other things that might fall.

2 Move away from exterior walls.

3 Face away from windows and glass.

4 Take shelter against your desk or a sturdy table.

5 Exit the building ASAP and get as far as possible from the source of the explosion. Do not use the elevators.

6 Monitor the news.

7 If the family needs to get back together and local phones do not work, communicate through an out-of-town contact: _____.

8 If phone lines are dead, the family will meet at _____ .

If in the Car

1 If there is an explosion or other factor that makes it difficult to control the vehicle, pull over. Stop the car and set the parking brake.

2 Get as far away as possible from the source of the explosion.

3 Avoid overpasses, bridges, power lines, signs, and other hazards if the explosion could impact the stability of the roadway.

4 If a power line falls on your car, you are at risk of electrical shock. Stay inside until a trained person removes the wire.

5 Monitor the news.

CHEMICAL OR BIOLOGICAL ATTACK

If You Think You May Have Been Exposed to a Chemical

1 Strip immediately.

2 Wash with water and soap, if possible. Be sure not to scrub the chemical into your skin.

3 Seek emergency medical attention.

4 Call the Poison Control Hotline at 800-222-1222.

5 If a family member develops any symptoms you believe might be related to a chemical or biological attack, keep them as far from others as possible.

Signs of Chemical or Biological Threat

1 Many people suffering from:

Watery eyes

Twitching

Choking

Difficulty breathing

Loss of coordination

2 Many sick or dead birds, fish, or small animals.

If You See Signs of Chemical or Biological Attack

1 Cover your mouth and nose with layers of fabrics that can filter the air but still allow breathing. (For example, two to three layers of cotton such as a T-shirt, handkerchief, or towel.) Otherwise, several layers of tissue or paper towels may help.

2 Quickly try to define the impacted area and get away from it.

3 Find clean air quickly.

4 Get away from the impacted area! If you cannot get out of the building or find clean air without passing through the area where you see signs of a chemical attack, move as far away as possible from the source of the attack and shelter in place in a room with as few windows, doors, and air vents as possible.

5 Shelter in place.

- Turn off fans, air-conditioning, and forced-air heating systems in the house.

- Close and lock all doors and windows to the house.

- Take the Go Bag with you into the designated room, unless you have reason to believe it has been contaminated.

- Seal all windows, doors, and air vents in the room with plastic sheeting and duct tape (found in the Go Bag).

- Be prepared to improvise and use what you have on hand to seal gaps so that you create a barrier between yourself and any contamination.

6 Monitor the news and look for the following information:

- Are you in the group or area authorities consider to be in danger?

- What are the signs and symptoms of the disease or poisoning?

- Are medications or vaccines being distributed? Where? Who should get them?

- Where should you seek emergency medical care if you become sick?

NUCLEAR THREAT

If There Is Advance Warning of an Upcoming Attack

1 Monitor the news and check whether airports are operating.

2 If planes are flying, and you have advance warning, head to the nearest operating airport. If not, head as far away as possible from the area that is said to be targeted.

3 Do not pack anything other than passports, credit cards, and cash. Then lock the house, and leave immediately.

If There Is No Advance Warning of an Attack

1 Monitor the news.

2 Consider if you can get out of the area or if it would be better to go inside a building to limit the amount of radioactive material you are exposed to.

3 If you take shelter, go as far below ground as possible, though any shield or shelter will help protect from the immediate effects of the blast and the pressure wave.

4 Take the Go Bag with you into the designated room unless you have reason to believe it has been contaminated.

5 Shelter in place.

- Turn off fans, air-conditioning, and forced-air heating systems in the house.

- Close and lock all doors and windows to the house.

- Seal all windows, doors, and air vents in the room with plastic sheeting and duct tape (found in the Go Bag).

- Be prepared to improvise and use what you have on hand to seal gaps so that you create a barrier between yourself and any contamination.

- To avoid radiation, cover your mouth and nose with layers of fabric that can filter the air but still allow breathing (for example, two to three layers of cotton such as a T-shirt, handkerchief, or towel. Otherwise, several layers of tissue or paper towels may help).

6 To limit the amount of radiation you are exposed to, think about shielding, distance, and time:

- Shielding: If you have a thick shield between yourself and the radioactive materials, more of the radiation will be absorbed by the shield, and you will be exposed to less.

- Distance: The farther away you are from the blast and the fallout, the lower your exposure.

- Time: Minimizing the time spent exposed will also reduce your risk.

7 Listen for official news as it becomes available.

8 If you think you have been exposed to radiation, take off your clothes and wash as soon as possible.

EMERGENCY

9 Wash with water and soap, if possible, being sure not to scrub any suspected substance into your skin.

10 Call the Poison Control Hotline at 800-222-1222.

11 If the family needs to get back together and local phones do not work, communicate through an out-of-town contact: _____.

12 If phone lines are dead, family will meet at _____ (out-of-town location).

EMERGENCY

ACKNOWLEDGMENTS (apologies for list form, but hey, this is a list book!)

1. There are three people who made this book turn from dream to reality: my cousin Nickie Greene; my agent, Andrea Barzvi; and my dearest friend's grandmother, Fifi Oscard. Nickie and Andrea, you believed in me. Fifi, you defied me to do better. Without all of you this book would never have happened.

2. Georgia, you gave me my voice. Not sure if I would have gone through with this book if you hadn't said yes. Seriously.

3. Sandi, everyone told me you were the greatest. And they were right! And I hope you will share your secret of how you make it look so easy.

4. Angelique, Beth, Jane, Sasha—you are the best friends anyone could ask for.

5. I would also like to thank the many friends and people I met along the way who knowingly, and

some unknowingly, contributed to the actual content of this overwhelming project (listed alphabetically by first name—the only way I keep my contacts, in case you were wondering):

Adam Glassman, Adrienne Eure, Alexandra Penney, Allison Chalfin, Aliza Pressman, Amanda Haan, Amanda Ross, Amy Glickman, Amy Harris, Andrea Topper, Angelique Kouris, Beatrice Novobaczky, Beth Murphy, Bill Weinpahl, Bill White, Brett Miles, Bryan Eure, Candace Corelli, Chip Lehrer, Chris Jennings, CJ Bouscaud, Cy O'Neal, David Rubin, Deanna Bedoya, Deborah Grubman, Dr. Mom, Ed Fogarty, Eli Tirosh, Elizabeth Harrison, Erin Gray, Evelyn Carr-White, Evelyn Webber, Gary DePersia, Gayle Bari, Gloria Nakash, Hamilton South, Hank Jorgensen, Husein Jafferjee, Holly Newman, Jaci Reid, Jae Portman, James Haigney, Jane Hoffman, Jason Possumato, Jean Kunhardt, Jeff Francis, Jeffrey Podolsky, Jenny Lethbridge, Jill Kargman, Joe Zee, Josh Lehrer, Jonathan Ehrlich, Judith Hidasi, Julie Chen, Kate Betts, Katie Lee Joel, Keith Green, Kelly Sugarman, Ken Slotnick, Kobi Halperin, Lara Logan, Larri Acevedo, Leslie Brille, Lewis Kohl, Libby Karmely, Lorraine Leckie, Mara Landis, Marcia Firshein, Marissa Rodriguez, Martha Stewart, Mary Portman, Maura Martin, Maikhu Gurung, Mukihya Gurung, Michael Shvo, Mickey Drexler, Mike Nichols, Nancy Freed, Neal Kotin, Nickie Greene, Paul Pearson, Peter Warren, Ramona Brodsky, Reid Price, Renee Saroff Oliner, Richard Firshein, Richard Pyles, Robert Kutnick, Rob Glatter, Robert Leviathan, Roland Davis, Ron Frasch, Roni Selig, Samantha Boardman, Sandi

Mendelson, Sarah Charles, Sasha Galantic, Shai Levy, Simon Doonan, Simone Levinson, Susie Block, Suzanne Stromfeld, Tom Flynn, Vanessa O'Connell, Virginia Smith, Wendi Murdoch, Yosi Tahari, and of course, the best for last . . . Seal.

6. To everyone at Simon & Schuster, especially Emily Westlake and Jennifer Robinson, but most important, Jennifer Bergstrom. You are the best.

7. Barbara Portman—thank you for your endless effort in editing this book.

8. Madonna—thank you for telling me to get back on the horse.

Your Lists

Your Lists

Your Lists

Your Lists

Your Lists

Your Lists